CHURCH ESSAYS.

BY

GEORGE CUMMING McWHORTER,

AUTHOR OF A "POPULAR HAND-BOOK OF THE NEW TESTAMENT."

PRODESSE ECCLESIA.

NEW YORK:
D. APPLETON AND COMPANY,
443 & 445 BROADWAY.
LONDON: 16 LITTLE BRITAIN.
1864.

TO

WOOTTON WRIGHT HAWKES,

PROFESSOR OF BELLES-LETTRES, TRINITY COLLEGE, HARTFORD,

IN APPRECIATION OF

HIS VARIED TALENTS AND ATTAINMENTS,

THESE ESSAYS ARE INSCRIBED

BY HIS FRIEND

THE AUTHOR.

PREFACE.

The Essays here collected, except those on Charity, Prayer, Death, appeared, during the years 1861 and 1862, in the "Church Monthly Magazine," Boston. They are published in the present shape with the assent of the Rev. Dr. Huntington, formerly senior editor of the "Church Monthly," to whom I am indebted for kindly favoring my purpose of giving these Essays a more permanent form. I trust they will not be found deficient in unity. "Our best and surest road to knowledge," says Lord Kaimes, "is by profiting by the knowledge (i. e. the reading) of others." Certainly it is the shortest — to some it is the only road. I hope, therefore, that these Essays, brief though they be, will prove advantageous to those who may chance to peruse them, and thus "read by deputy."

G. C. McW.

CONTENTS.

O God, who didst teach the hearts of thy faithful people, by sending to them the light of thy Holy Spirit; grant us by the same Spirit to have a right judgment in all things, through Christ Jesus our Saviour, who liveth and reigneth with Thee in the unity of the same Spirit, one God, world without end. *Amen.*

THE LITURGY.

The Liturgy may seem a trite subject,—one which has been wellnigh exhausted,—but it is so deeply seated in the hearts of all true Church people, that a few more words in reference to it, we trust, will not be without interest. Perhaps, too, the affection of some of our readers for the service may exceed their knowledge of what they love. In order, therefore, to increase the one, and enlarge the other, we add our voice to those which have been already raised to do honor to one of the chief treasures of the Protestant Church.

Whence comes this noble formula of devotion?—"the diction of which," says Lord Macaulay, "has directly or indirectly contributed to form the diction of almost every great English writer, and has extorted the admiration of the most accomplished infidels and of the most accomplished nonconformists, of such men as David Hume and Robert Hall." We have heard it asserted, and it is commonly believed among the uninformed, that the Church of England, the immediate progenitor of the Church in this country, is merely the Roman Church reformed. With equal truth, and with an equal share of reading, it is often claimed, that the Prayer Book bears the same relation to the Missal. Now, what is the truth in regard to these two points? Let us briefly examine.

At the time Christianity became the religion of the Roman world, the Empire, for its more convenient government, was distributed into fourteen Dioceses, of which the Eastern and Western sections contained seven each. These Dioceses were subdivided into one hundred and eighteen Eparchates, and the latter again into numerous Precincts. Christianity, it will be remembered, was then embodied in the Church Catholic,—we use the word in its exact sense,—all Christians were then members of the one body, and through it drank into the one Spirit. Very naturally, the Church, as soon as possible, adapted herself to the civil disposition of the Empire, and became similarly distributed. Thus the Church was divided into fourteen Dioceses, each of which was presided over by a Patriarch or Archbishop; the Dioceses were subdivided into Provinces under the government of Metropolitans; and these again into Parishes under the rule of Bishops. The Parishes also were sometimes further subdivided; hence the Chorepiscopi. According to the Jus Cyprium,—a canon passed at the Council of Ephesus, A. D. 431, the third of the four great councils whose decrees Gregory the Great declared to be worthy of the highest veneration,

—no Bishop can lawfully *episcopize* out of his own territory. Some refer this canon to the injunction of St. Peter, 1st iv. 15, "Let none of you suffer as an *allotrio-episcopos.*" Perhaps the reference is just; however that may be, the canon is certainly founded in reason.

For six centuries, the Bishops of the Church were equal, differing only in the extent and importance of their respective territories. Of course, the Archbishops of the Dioceses exceeded them in ability and distinction, and among these the Patriarchs of Rome and Constantinople were preëminent. The Apostles, whose mantles fell upon the Bishops,* were equal in dignity, authority, and we may add humility. Peter may have had a *primacy*, but no *supremacy;* for St. Paul declares that he himself was "not a whit behind the chiefest of the apostles." Gregory the Great, too, asserts distinctly, that "whoever shall arrogate to himself the title of Universal Bishop is the precursor of Antichrist." Notwithstanding, in the year 606,—a number not far removed from the number of the Beast, Rev. xiii. 18,—Boniface, Bishop of Rome, assumed the title and office of Universal Bishop, thus "lording it over God's heritage" in defiance of the injunctions of him of whom he professed to hold, and in fact *attorning* to the Adversary. Phocas, the Emperor, however, desirous that Rome should have the precedence in all

* "We require you to find out *one* Church upon *the face of the whole earth* that hath not been ordained by Episcopal regimen since the time that the blessed Apostles were here conversant."—HOOKER.

things, spiritual as well as temporal, sustained and furthered Boniface in his usurpation. Hence the Papacy, and the consequent "woe" to the world.

At quite an early date, most likely in the apostolic age, the Church was planted in Britain. The normal features were exactly the same as those of the older sister Churches. The British Church was, therefore, a regular, organized branch of the Church Catholic, and vested with all the rights incident thereto. When Augustine, A. D. 596, arrived in Britain, on a mission from Gregory, Bishop of Rome, to convert the supposed pagan island, he found there the Church,—a Church as old as that of the See of Rome. Instead, however, of aiding the British Church and endeavoring to strengthen and develop her, as he was bound by law and charity to do, he immediately got himself made Archbishop of Canterbury by Ethelbert, King of Kent, and proceeded to subdue the British Church and render her tributary to Rome. Now, the authority of the Bishop of Rome did not cover all Italy, much less Britain. Hence the act of Gregory was clearly a violation of the *Jus Cyprium.* Besides, Augustine,—who did not derive his orders from the Roman Church, but from the Church in Gaul, whose orders are traceable to the Greek Church,—as soon as he became Archbishop of Canterbury, was debarred from attorning in any way to Rome. It was not only a craven act, but a manifest violation of the trust involved in his office. Notwithstanding, Augustine did not hesitate to play the part which Gregory had set down for him, base though it was. Consequently, in place of comforting the British Church, he made war upon her as soon as he obtained a foothold for his operations. In this manner, the Roman Church, contrary to law, forced her way into Britain, and laid the foundation of her future power and eventual disgrace in that island. It should not be forgotten that most of the Saxons whom Augustine converted within twenty years after his visit relapsed into paganism. Yet, the organization which he introduced was not lost. The old British Church, too, still lived on, principally in Wales, preserving her sound form and pure faith. As time went on, however, the Roman Church succeeded in overlaying the British Church to so great a degree that the latter became completely obscured. In truth, it might be said of her as of Eneas:

> "Obscure she went through dreary shades, that led
> Along the waste dominions of the dead."

The Papal Church also obtained some recognitions from the Government of England which greatly strengthened her hands. However, the British Church did not despair, or succumb without "opposition to the Papal encroachments." "Protests," says Dr. Wordsworth, "were made by Egfrid, King of Northumberland, and by his successor, King Alfrid, on occasion of the first great appeal to Rome; by King Edward the Confessor, by Henry the First, and succeeding sovereigns;

and the same spirit which dictated these remonstrances declared itself publicly and legislatively in the *Constitutions of Clarendon*, A. D. 1164; and again A. D. 1246; in the *Statute of Carlisle*, A. D. 1297; in the *Articles of the Clergy*, in the *Statutes of Provisors*, A. D. 1350–'63–'89; of *Mortmain* and of *Præmunire*, A. D. 1391–'2; and, finally, in the Statutes of Henry VIII., from A. D. 1531 to 1543, which, in the opinion of the soundest English lawyers, were not *operative* but *declaratory* acts; that is, they were *no new* laws, but only vindicated and enforced *the old*." * But, in spite of her resistance, the British, or more properly, the English, Church, fell into a state of absolute servitude to Rome, and, with the *pallium* of the latter, received the usually attendant share of corruption. Fortunately, though humbled, she was not destroyed.

Such was the sad position of the Church of England when the revival of learning and the Reformation shed new light upon the scene and changed the aspect of the world. "The morning star" of the latter movement, says Professor Eadie, "was WYCLIFFE. In the latter part of the fourteenth century he preached a species of Protestantism,—denying transubstantiation and the supremacy of the Pope, and severely condemning

* SHAKSPEARE, speaking through the mouth of King John, says:

"No Italian priest
Shall tithe or toll in our dominions.
So tell the Pope; all reverence set apart
To him and his usurped authority."

See King John, Act III.

the abuse of her temporalities on the part of the Church." Though he did not win the crown of martyrdom, like Huss and Jerome, and did not live to see the errors which he opposed corrected, "he will ever be remembered," continues the Professor, "as a good and great man, an advocate of ecclesiastical independence, an unquailing foe to Popish tyranny, a translator of Scripture into our mother tongue, and an industrious instructor of the people in their own rude, but ripening dialect."

The seed, however, which Wycliffe planted, finally sprang up and bore fruit a thousand-fold. In the sixteenth century the flood of the Reformation spread over Europe. On the Continent, the Reformers swept away the Church, while in Great Britain, the Church took the lead, and reformed, or rather restored, herself. Thus the Bishops of the Church, under God, aided by Henry VIII.,—a man bad indeed and impelled by selfish motives, but who doubtless acted, like Nebuchadnezzar, *judicially*,*—Edward VI., and Elizabeth, led forth the Church from her Egyptian bondage and Egyptian darkness into liberty and light. They preserved in her all that was sound and primitive, reformed what was amiss, and presented her at last a witness to the world, right in order, perfect in faith, pure in practice, Catholic in truth, and Protestant against error,—

* It has been well said, that God never uses *good* men to pull down or *bad* men to build up. Thus, Henry was an instrument of judgment,—Cranmer and his followers ministers of mercy.

in a word, the National Church of England, intact as when first overshadowed and defiled by the schismatic power of Rome. Precisely as has been aptly said, Job was the same "upright" Job after the "sore boils" were removed that he was before he was "afflicted." "Where," said the proud and insolent Bonner, with a sneer, to good old Hugh Latimer, "where was your Church before Luther's time?" "Where your grace's face was this morning before it was washed," keenly retorted the latter. Yes, the Church of England ever has been, in all ages, under all phases, through evil and good report, the "never-forsaken" National Church of England,—the bulwark of Christianity,—and an integral member of the "One Holy Catholic and Apostolic Church." Of this honor she is justly careful, for it is a "derivative" from her to hers.

We hope to make it equally clear, that the Liturgy of the Church of England, and consequently of our own Church, is no more "a rag of Popery" than the Church herself, and that, like her, in the words of Jeremy Taylor, "it is as ancient and primitive as it is pious and unblamable."

As soon as the Church had become sufficiently established in the world, the Apostles and their successors, for the sake of propriety and convenience, and the furtherance of devotion, introduced formulas of worship. This course was extremely natural, inasmuch as the primitive Churches had before their eyes the well-known customs of the Jews, who, from the first, it is evident, made use of forms. The Temple service was, undoubtedly, the grandest exhibition of divine worship that the world has ever witnessed. Apart from the sacrificial offices and rites, Moses and the Prophets were read, liturgical prayers were offered, the Psalms of David were chanted,—be it remembered, in the sublime old Hebrew,—to the sound of many and various musical instruments, by the twenty-four courses of trained singers, and the people were blessed in words prescribed by the Lord himself. In the synagogues, also, forms were used. The latter, probably, did not differ materially from those employed by the Jews at the present day. Doubtless they were not the same exactly in every synagogue, just as they are not so now. The *Affirmation*, which may be said to correspond with our *Gloria Patri*, has, unquestionably, always formed a part of every Jewish service. We allude here to the "*Shama, shama Yisrael, Elohika Eloi echad*,"—"Hear, O Israel, the Lord thy God is one Lord." No one acquainted with the language can hear the solemn strain now without emotion.

Besides the practice of the Jews,—of whom came Salvation, that is, Christ,—the early Christians had for their guidance, not only the example of the great forerunner, John, who taught his disciples to pray, but that of our Saviour, who gave his followers the perfect prayer which is called by his name. The petitions in the Lord's Prayer, it is well known, are to be found almost literally in the Jewish liturgy. The ascription at the end of the Prayer in St. Matthew's Gospel, we may add, is now conceded to be without sufficient MS. authority. It probably was interpolated into the text from some old liturgy. Our Saviour, likewise, aside from his use of the Psalms and Jewish forms, as Dr. Hook observes, when in the garden having occasion to pray three times to the same effect, according to St. Matthew, used ever the *same words*. How touching an argument to the Christian for a "form of sound words"!

We have said that forms of devotion were employed by the Christians at an early date. The use of the Psalms of David as hymns of praise and thanksgiving came naturally to all who had been Jews, and was continued as a matter of course. Our Saviour and his disciples, without doubt, sang the *Great Hallel*—Psalms 115 to 118 inclusive—at every Paschal Feast, for it was the Passover Hymn; and the Apostles availed themselves of the Psalms, when they lifted up their voices "with one accord." But the Lord's Prayer, which could not have been omitted on any occasion of either private or public worship, must be regarded as the centre from which all forms of Christian worship have radiated. It is worthy of notice here, that wherever forms of prayer have been adopted, the Lord's Prayer has always preserved the first place, and only among those who pride themselves upon extempore efforts, is it fallen into desuetude, and the anomaly shown to the world, of a congregation ostensibly assembled in the name of the Lord, without praying to their Divine Master in the words which he commanded his followers to use; on the contrary, praying intentionally in other words, and often not even in his name.

It is thought that the Apostles or Bishops of the several Churches arranged, at first, each one for his own people, a formula of devotion. In all probability they varied in language and expression, though they agreed in purport and design. The earliest forms were, doubtless, offices for the two sacraments. In fact, the Creed can be traced to the declaration made at Baptism; while *Liturgy* was originally the name of the Eucharistic service. Of course, the Sacraments are the centre of the Church in all respects. "The apostolical canons, however," says Dr. Hook, "mention some set forms of prayer, both before and after the Communion." This was after the Church had begun more fully to develop herself. When she had obtained a position in the world, extended religious services came into vogue. According to Palmer ("Origines Liturgicæ"), there were four great primitive Liturgies, namely, 1. *The Oriental Liturgy*, which prevailed from the Euphrates to the Hellespont, and from the latter to the southern extremity of Greece, and which was generally attributed to St. James; 2. *The Alexandrian Liturgy*, which from remote antiquity has been the liturgy of Egypt, Abyssinia, and the country proximate to the Mediterranean Sea, westward, which was known as St. Mark's; 3. *The Roman Liturgy*, which prevailed over Italy, Sicily, and the diocese of Africa, and which was credited to St. Peter; 4. *The Gallican Liturgy*, which was long used in Ephesus, Gaul, and Spain, and which was ascribed to St. John. That the Apostles referred to had any part in the composition of the above liturgies is unsustained by adequate proof. The one by St. James, "though greatly interpolated," says Foulkes, "and a model of all subsequent liturgies, is by some considered genuine." Among these liturgies there was a general agreement. They could not differ with respect to matters of faith and order. It is not to be supposed, however, that the Churches where they prevailed confined themselves entirely to them. Undoubtedly, variations were made and new prayers were introduced, either to suit the taste of those in authority, or to conform to what circumstances might seem to require; for a perfect liturgy was not made in a day nor in a generation. Besides, St. Basil and St. Chrysostom, in the fourth century, were both authors of forms of devotion. Every one is acquainted with the beautiful prayer taken from the liturgy of the latter, and incorporated into our service. The Te Deum, too, the most sublime of uninspired hymns,—thought by many to have been composed by St. Ambrose in honor of the Holy Trinity, on the occasion of the baptism of St. Augustine, but which is also attributed to others,—is another example to the same purpose. St. Basil and St. Chrysostom seem to have seen apostolic liturgies. Perhaps they were those which we have said have been ascribed to St. John and St. James. Thus it is a reasonable conclusion from all we read, that the Fathers of the Church, from the earliest time, were in the habit of composing prayers, hymns, and devotional services wherewith to honor God and his Christ. Indeed, everything goes to prove to every candid mind that forms of worship were the rule throughout the early Church; and it is not unfair to say that the habit of extemporizing is as modern as the bodies that employ it.

The Liturgies of the Eastern portion of the Church were principally in the Greek language, though not exclusively so. Sometimes they were adapted to the vernacular of the people, whatever that might be. The Western Liturgies were, as far as we know, all in Latin. The chief one,—the one which finally displaced the Gallican and every other within its reach,—was the Roman. We will briefly consider this. Originally, it was distributed throughout a number of books. These were divided, according to Palmer, into two classes:

FIRST CLASS.

1. The *Antiphonarium*, or responsive service, including anthems.
2. The *Hymnarium*, or metrical hymns.
3. The *Collectarium*, or concluding collects.
4. The *Homelarium*, *Passionarium*, and *Martyrologium*, which need no explanation.

SECOND CLASS.

1. The *Sacramentary*, comprising prayers and collects, principally for the Communion.

2. The *Lectionary*, Lessons from the Old and New Testaments, the Commandments, the Epistles (or Apostle), and Gospels.

Subordinate to this was the *Evangelistorium*, or the Gospels.

3. The *Antiphonary*, containing the Offertory and Communion anthems.

Such was the character of the early Roman Liturgy. About the twelfth century, the books of the second class were revised, and condensed into one volume, which was henceforth known as the *Missal*, or Mass Book. Later, by a decree of the Council of Trent, the books of the first class were likewise revised and formed into one volume, which was established by the Bull of Pius V. in 1566 as the *Breviary*. Having become "depraved," it was revised by Clement VIII. in 1602, and again finally by Urban VIII. in 1631. Besides the above, there is another book, termed the *Ritual*, which contains various religious offices. These three works comprise the Liturgy proper of the Church of Rome.* In addition, however, she has three minor liturgies, namely, the *Ceremoniale*, for the use of the Pope alone; the *Pontificate*, for the Bishops; and the *Pastorale*, for the

* The *Breviary* corresponds substantially with our Morning and Evening Prayer; the *Missal* with the Communion service; the *Ritual* with the other offices of the Prayer Book.—SHEPHERD.

inferior clergy. It is almost needless to add that *all* the Roman books are deeply tinctured with the corruptions of the Papal system.

The early British Church harmonized with the Eastern or Greek Church, as is evident from her having observed Easter according to the usage of the latter. Originally, we learn from Bede, she had a liturgy derived from primitive sources, and adapted to her purposes. Subsequently, she is supposed to have received the Gallican Liturgy, in addition, from her nearest and more learned neighbor, whose assistance she had invoked during the Pelagian controversy. Augustine, when he undertook to regulate matters in the British Church, by the advice of Gregory, framed a new liturgy from what seemed good to him in any Church, and prescribed that to the English. "This liturgy of St. Augustine continued," writes Dr. Hook, "for some ages, till Osmond, Bishop of Sarum and Chancellor of England, A. D. 1078, finding that new prayers and offices abounded everywhere, reduced them all to one form, and from thence it was called *secundum usum Sarum*." Although the "Uses of Sarum" obtained generally throughout England, Wales, and Ireland, there were other "Uses," namely, the Uses of York, Hereford, Bangor, and Lincoln. These were free, according to Palmer, from the gross corruptions which later disfigured the Romish Ritual. There were, also, other forms of worship extant in England and Scotland, arising from the disposition of the Bishops to arrange services, each in his own diocese, to suit his own taste. In the main, however, they were alike, as they, doubtless, all came from the same fountains. As we find no evidence of any effort having been made to harmonize fully the worship of the Church throughout England, it is apparent that, in the sixteenth century, the rites, ceremonies, and services must have been numerous, and to some extent various. It must be acknowledged, also, that in many parts they had become corrupted by the prevailing influence of Rome, and tainted by her errors. We come now to the Reformation.

When the Spirit of Truth wrought in the Church in England, and it was determined to purge her from the sins that had crept into her, and restore her to her pristine purity and position, it became all-important to reform the liturgies. At that time, in disregard of St. Paul's injunction concerning "unknown tongues," (1 Cor. xiv.), the services were all in Latin. To correct this grievous error, and enable the people to worship God in their own language, was deemed of primary necessity. Only so could "all things be done to edifying." Inspired, therefore, by such motives, the Convocation which was in session, A. D. 1537, published the "Bishop's Book" or, "The godly and pious Institution of a Christian Man." It comprised the Lord's Prayer, the Hail Mary, the Creed, Ten Commandments, and Seven Sacraments. In 1540 it was republished, altered and improved, with the title of "A necessary Doctrine and Erudition for any Chrysten Man." The process of reform, it will be perceived, was gradual or formative. Notwithstanding, a large step was taken in the year 1545. Then, the "King's Primer,"—framed by a committee of bishops and learned doctors, appointed five years previously by Henry VIII.—was put forth. The "Primer" contained Morning and Evening Prayer in the vulgar tongue, and is, says Dr. Hook, "not very different from our Common Prayer."

Shortly after the accession of Edward VI., in 1548, a full Liturgy for the Church was compiled and published by authority. It is commonly known as the "*First* Book of Edward VI.," and resembles the present Prayer Book. At the instance of Cranmer, however, it was revised and republished in 1551, and is called the "*Second* Book of Edward VI." The alterations made by the latter were, in some, though not in all respects, a great improvement. Nevertheless, they were said to proceed from "curiosity rather than any worthy cause." Both, it ought to be remembered, were free from Romish error. We have now to record the reaction which took place on the death of Edward.

Mary ascended the throne in 1553. During her terrible reign, the Church saw herself deprived of her rights, despoiled of her Liturgy, forced back again into the arms of Rome, and martyred in the persons of some of her noblest sons. Fortunately for the cause of true religion, fortunately for the world, the reign of Mary was short.

Elizabeth succeeded her sister in 1558, and without

delay caused the Church to be restored to her rightful position. As soon as possible, too, a Liturgy, revised from the two Books of Edward, was published. This continued in use during the lifetime of Elizabeth.

James I. followed the queen in 1603. The same year, a conference between the representatives of the Church, the king, and some distinguished dissenters, was held at Hampton Court. The result of this interview was, that the Liturgy was again revised and, we may add, improved.

Nothing was done in the reign of Charles I. During the pendency of the Commonwealth, however, the Church was again deprived of her rights, and remained in that position until the Restoration, when she received her own again.

After the accession of Charles II., in 1661, when the Church once more stood in her true place, conferences were held at the house of the Bishop of London, in the Savoy,—a section of the town which once claimed to possess peculiar privileges, somewhat similar to Alsatia, which our readers have read about in the "Fortunes of Nigel." At these conferences, Churchmen, Presbyterians, and Puritans were all present. As the dissenters, however, wished to annihilate the Church, and Baxter was conceited enough to imagine that he could make a liturgy superior to any the Church had ever had, the conferees agreed to nothing. Nevertheless, good came from these interviews; for, in consequence of some suggestions on the part of certain Episcopal members, a Convocation was held the ensuing May, when the Liturgy was again revised. "In a word," says Dr. Hook, "the whole Liturgy was then brought to the state in which it now stands, and was unanimously subscribed by both houses of convocation on Friday, December 20, 1661; and being brought to the House of Lords the March following, both houses very readily passed an act for its establishment.'

Such, in brief, were the steps taken by the Church of England in the construction of her Liturgy. It will be seen that its formation was gradual,—many years elapsing ere it was perfected,—and that it was intimately interwoven with the renovation and restoration of the Church herself. The mode pursued in its compilation was as follows: the Bishops and other Divines to whom the duty was intrusted had before them all the liturgies extant; but instigated, as Casaubon has remarked, by a "love for truth and a love for antiquity," they collated the most ancient liturgies, and out of them framed a Liturgy primitive in formula and language, and scriptural in fact. Besides the Articles of Religion, nothing new was introduced, except what the lapse of time and change in manners demanded, and what was necessary to render the work operative. The compilation was initiated and carried through by the Church. It was strictly a Church movement and work. Martin Bucer and Peter Martyr, it is true, advised with Cranmer, upon the revision of the "First Book of Edward VI." The Continental reformers were not then unfriendly to the Church of England. On the contrary, the soundness of her ecclesiastical polity was conceded by Luther, Melancthon, Beza, and Calvin. Indeed, the latter addressed a letter to Edward VI. on the subject of obtaining the episcopate from the Church of England for the Church of Geneva. Unfortunately, the letter fell into the hands of Gardner and Bonner, who jesuitically replied in the name of the Church, repelling Calvin's overtures, and thus frustrating his efforts to get the Church established in her integrity on the Continent.

Cranmer doubtless derived assistance from the suggestions of Bucer and Martyr. They were good men. We have already said that the "*Second* Book of Edward VI." was in many respects an improvement on the *first*.

The Dissenters likewise assisted at the Hampton Court Conference. The alterations made in the Liturgy then were few; but they were important, and not such as would have commended themselves to the opponents of the Church. At the Savoy Conference the Dissenters were also represented. Their efforts, however, were confined to weak attempts either to emasculate or destroy the Liturgy, rather than to improve it. Happily, they utterly failed in their design. Happily for the Church of England, "Her spirit-stirring Liturgy, and a scrupulous adherence to it, has, under God, notwithstanding the mutations of men and things, and all the aspersions cast upon her, as coldness, formality, and a want of evangelical feeling: we say, *a scrupulous* adherence to her Liturgy has preserved her integrity, beyond any denomination of Christians since the Reformation."*

The Savoy Conference was the last opportunity afforded the Dissenters of interfering in the matter. The final revision, which took place in the year 1661, was made by the Convocation of the Church herself, legally assembled. Thus, as has been before insisted, the Prayer Book is a Church work, and one of which she is justly proud.

We have now shown, we think, that the reformation *in* the Church of England and the renovation of her Liturgy were no revolution, but a restoration of what was ancient and accepted, and a return to what was pure and primitive.

Let us also cast our eyes upon our own country. How stands the matter here?

The colonies were nearly all planted by Englishmen; hence many of the latter must have been, at least nominally, churchmen. The religious state of the colonies was far from good. Indeed, so indifferent was it, that it, at last, excited attention, and even compunction, in the mother country. In 1661, commissaries were sent to Virginia and Maryland to take charge of matters, and efforts were initiated to supply the plantations with lawful ministers. Subsequently, at the instance of Lord Clarendon, Dr. Murray was appointed

* Religious Intelligencer (Dutch Reformed); see Bishop Odenheimer's "Origin of Common Prayer."

Bishop of Virginia by Charles II. The death of the latter, however, frustrated the appointment. We are not aware that the Doctor was ever consecrated. The number of the clergymen of the Establishment in all the colonies was small even in the latter part of the seventeenth century, and they were not well provided for. Such was the position of the Church in the colonies, when the Society for the Propagation of the Gospel was inaugurated, in the year 1701. The latter immediately extended its fostering hand over America; and to the efforts of that venerable society, under God, are due the preservation and propagation of the Church in the colonial period of our history. Surrounded by active enemies, without the aid of the Society, perhaps, she might have died. The evil lay in the want of bishops. So deeply was the deprivation felt, that "letters and memorials from the colonies supply, for a whole century," says Wilberforce, "a connected chain of expostulations; yet still the mother country was deaf to their entreaties. At home they were reëchoed from many quarters. Succeeding archbishops pressed them on successive administrations; and the Society for the Propagation of the Gospel, during almost every year, made some effort in the same cause." In 1738, we find the Bishop of London and others "laboring much but in vain with court and ministry" on this subject. During Walpole's administration, "memorials from all parts of the continent were sent home," praying that bishops might be given them. But they produced no effect. The cold-hearted minister was dead to everything connected with religion. Every entreaty failed. The Church was not permitted to grant the boon her children craved, and they languished in consequence; but through no fault of hers. She did what she could. Let the responsibility rest upon those who hindered her in the execution of her duty.

Unable to obtain bishops legally, in this extremity, the step thus described by Wilberforce suggested itself. "The bishops who had been deprived of their temporalities for refusing to take the oath of allegiance to William III. did not thereby lose their spiritual character. They had still, therefore, the power of conferring holy orders, and of consecrating other bishops by the laying on of hands, although their doing so was plainly 'irregular and schismatical.' This step, unhappily, they took, at the risk of entailing a fearful schism on the English Church. Having founded a counter-episcopate at home, they could feel little scruple in granting to America that boon which England had so long and so unwarrantably withheld from her. It was therefore natural that some of the American clergy should look to them for succor, and that they should lend a favorable ear to their requests. Accordingly, Dr. Welton, and Mr. Talbot, the oldest missionary of the Society for the Propagation of the Gospel, solicited and received consecration from the non-juring bishops: Dr. Welton was consecrated by Dr. Ralph Taylor in 1722, and Mr. Talbot shortly afterward by Drs. Taylor and Welton.

Political disqualifications made them unable to perform publicly any Episcopal acts ; but there is reason to believe that they privately administered the rite of Confirmation, and at least in some cases ordained clergy." No adequate practical benefit, therefore, resulted from this ill-advised step. Still it manifests how great was the anxiety to obtain the episcopate for America, and of what importance it was regarded by those interested.

Affairs continued in the same position until after the Revolution. Meanwhile the Church, shorn of her powers, and necessarily retarded in her growth, was kept alive by the efforts of the Society for the Propagation of the Gospel. After the colonies had achieved their independence, at an early period, the churchmen of the country instituted measures whereby the Church in America might assume her true and rightful position in the eyes of the world. We need not particularize the steps that were taken to effect the object. Suffice it to say, that bishops were obtained from the Church of England, and the Episcopal Church of Scotland,—who derived her orders from the former,—and after some unavoidable delays, in 1789, the year the Constitution of the United States went into effect, the Church was organized in the new-born nation. The first work of the first convention of the Church was, says Mr. Evans, "to revise and adopt the Prayer Book. They settled the book very nearly as it now is; only the offices for Consecrating, Ordaining, and Instituting, and the Thirty-Nine Articles, have since been added; the former in 1792, and the latter in 1801." In 1808, the Constitution was amended so as to give a *full negative* to the House of Bishops in the legislation of the convention. Since that time, the Church in the United States, though properly not established as an organ of the Government, as she is in England, nor deprived of her true position, as she is in Scotland, but independent, and about her Master's business, has stood forth as the lawful representative in this nation of the Church of the Apostles, duly and canonically organized in conformity with Scripture and primitive usage.

The Liturgy of the American Church was compiled from the Prayer Book of the Church of England and the old Scottish Prayer Book. In the revision, some things were omitted, what was best in each retained, and what was necessary to adapt the new book to the institutions of the country was supplied. Space forbids us to go into an analysis of the American Prayer Book. In matters of faith, order, and practice, it does not differ from the English and Scottish books; while in point of merit, as a whole, we believe we state a common opinion, when we say that it is superior to either.

Our theme has been the Liturgy. Connected, as it is, with the life and progress of the Church, in considering its origin and development, we have been unavoidably led into a comprehensive view of the latter. In the course pursued, we have shown that we have a perfect branch of the apostolic Church, adorned by a "form of sound words,"—words which, when not Scripture itself, are the faithful reflex of it, and which, if "*held fast*," will never fail to insure the Church's freedom from "false doctrine, heresy, and schism." It is not our purpose to indulge in a prolonged eulogy of the Prayer Book. Since Cranmer's day, the "Godly Book" has been honored by the praises of the wisest and best of men. No one that has any knowledge in him doubts that it is the first of uninspired compositions. We will only, in addition, express the earnest hope that it will continue to be the noble vehicle whereby the Church in Great Britain and America shall continue, in spirit and in truth, to worship the FATHER through the SON, until there shall be no more temple, and prayer shall be lost in praise.

THE TRINITY.

This subject has ever been regarded as the first doctrine, the chief mystery, of our holy religion. It underlies the whole of theology, and is necessary to the very existence of the Christian faith. Indeed, it is the main constituent of that faith. Without it, Christianity falls from its high estate as the religion of God, and becomes, instead, merely a religion of man. Without it the Church—the divinely ordained exponent of Christianity—is no longer the Church of God, but a device of man. A full belief in the Trinity is inseparable from the calling of a Christian, from the life of a Churchman, the true profession of the Catholic faith. The importance of this subject is obvious. The depth of the mystery cannot be overrated. We approach our subject, therefore, with reverence, not unmindful that it is not in the power of man to discover the hidden things of Deity, but only to develop what God has revealed. In such a spirit, and so far, we shall pursue our investigation of this wonderful mystery; and as we shall have truth for our guide and for our end, we hope that what we may say will be found neither uninteresting nor unprofitable. Let us come, then, to our subject directly.

Man cannot comprehend God. It is a principle, as true in mental as in physical science, that the contents must be smaller than that which contains. Hence, finite man cannot comprehend (*take in*) his infinite Maker. Yet he may conceive of Him. To aver that man cannot conceive of God, is to assume that, as far as he is concerned, there is no God. Now that there is a God, is evident from three undeniable proofs: First, from the internal revelation which God has made of Himself to the inner man; so that, from time immemorial, all nations have ever recognized the existence of a Supreme Being. Second, from the external revelation which God has made of Himself in His works; which works, exhibiting, as they do, plain evidences of design, affirm beyond question the existence of a designer—the Creator. Third, from the verbal revelation which God has made of Himself—the Bible—a revelation which has never been successfully impugned, and the very essence of which, even the "Westminster Review" admits to be "Truth."

We affirm, then, that God is; and though man cannot comprehend God, yet he can and does conceive of him.

But what is this conception? Man does not conceive of God in the abstract. God is not an idea, but a fact, or, rather, the Great Fact. Consequently, man must conceive of him in the concrete, and the conception must be susceptible of analysis and definition. In other words, the existence of God being demonstrated, what do we know of him?

We know that God is the one only self-existent Being, who possesses a sole, separate, indivisible nature peculiar to himself alone; and, in regard to which nature, everything that is, whether thought or entity, is external. God's nature is one. It is what we mean when we say the Deity—the God-head.

God comprehends in his nature three necessary incontrovertible terms, viz.: infinite Wisdom, infinite Goodness, infinite Power. They are absolutely necessary to a conception of God, we might say, to the existence of God; for God would not be God without them. Thus, infinite wisdom is necessary, that God may know all things aright; infinite goodness, that benevolence may harmonize with wisdom; infinite power, that the dictates of wisdom and goodness may be carried into effect. It is obvious that these three terms are requisite in finite proportions to the moral constitution of man, who was made in the "likeness" of God; hence they must exist in infinite proportions in the nature of God himself. They are necessary to his supremacy in every way.

God is often said to possess certain peculiar attributes, as omniscience, omnipresence, truth, justice, mercy, love, omnipotence. All these, however, are either different names for the three terms respectively, or are plain correlatives of them. Thus the first four are included in "wisdom"; the two following in "goodness"; while the last is a synonym of "power." These terms and their correlates belonging to the Divine nature, God is frequently said to be Wisdom, Goodness, Power. He is each and all; and all are one—Beauty. Similarly, the seven prismatic colors, on investigation, may be reduced to three. These three absolute, primitive colors united, form one ray of pure, white light. So the Divine nature; analyzed, it seems to be compound; but, like the pure ray, it is really one. God is Light.

We have said that the terms of God's nature are incontrovertible. It follows that God is limited by those terms. Thus God cannot err, for it would impugn his wisdom. But, we are often told, God is omnipotent—cannot he do anything? No. He cannot do what would controvert the terms of his existence, the moral elements of his own peculiar nature. For instance, God cannot cause $2 \times 2 = 5$. Why not? Because that $2 \times 2 = 4$ is a mathematical truth. All mathematical truth is a part of God's truth—the attribute of His wisdom. God has caused $2 \times 2 = 4$ because it is true. It is only a mode of expressing a truth. God must think the truth, and must carry out his thoughts. He could no more do otherwise than he could cease to exist. God's perfect nature is God's perfect law. He is the law unto Himself.

Again: Has God, in view of His peculiar nature, any necessary rule of action? Certainly. The affirmative follows as in the former case. God's nature being both perfect and infinite, His action must be spontaneous. God does not feel, then act; nor think, then act; nor feel and think, then act; but His infinite power instantly perfects the unerring dictates of His infinite wisdom and goodness. His purposes are from everlasting. Hence spontaneity is the rule of God's action. It is a consequence of His nature. He is the rule unto Himself.

So much, reason alone tells us of God. But God has made an express revelation of Himself in Holy Scripture. The latter not only confirms what we know from reason, but tells us much more. It tells us not only that there is one God, who is the only God, but that He is a Spirit, and that His indivisible, Divine Nature integrally occupies and informs three several Persons,—the Father, the Son, and the Holy Ghost. In the economy of God these Three Persons exercise three different offices, and are as distinctly three in their respective personalities as the Godhead that informs them is one in its unity. Triuneness is the eternal constitution of the Deity as it is revealed in Scripture, whence it has been epitomized in the creeds of the Church,—the symbols of Christianity. There is one God, and in the unity of the Godhead three Persons. The Trinity is one in the Unity, and the Unity is indivisible in the Trinity. This is the Catholic doctrine,—this is the proposition of the Trinity.

"Aristotle's similitude of a triangle comprehended in a square," says Sir Thomas Browne, "doth somewhat illustrate the trinity of our souls, and that the triple unity of God; for there is in us not three distinct souls, yet differing faculties, that can and do subsist apart in different subjects, and yet in us are thus united as to make but one soul and substance. If one soul were so perfect as to inform three distinct bodies, that were a *petty* trinity. Conceive the distinct number of three, not divided nor separated by the intellect, but actually comprehended in its unity, and that is a *perfect* trinity."

If it be remembered that the Godhead, as has been often written, is not only a singular and indivisible nature, but the Divine Nature, as capable, therefore, of informing three persons as one, yet necessarily one in itself, the truth as well as the Scripturalness of the proposition of the Trinity, as above stated, will be readily apprehended. Indeed, it is only when the proposition is misstated or confused that the doctrine of the Trinity becomes an *opprobrium mentis*, an offence, and rejected of men. If searchers after truth would sincerely endeavor to inform themselves distinctly as to just what the Church requires them to believe, they would avoid many difficulties, and find fewer obstacles to surmount in their upward path. Nay, if a reasonable effort were made on the part of Christians always clearly to apprehend all the great doctrines of their profession, the latter would be always held really, and not merely verbally, as they too often are, by those even who should be able to give a reason for the faith which they confess with their lips. Perhaps it may be doubted whether one actually does believe what he simply repeats without understanding. Thus discussions of the deep things of God have been productive of good; for, by the evolution of truth, many who were unwittingly in darkness have been brought to the light. It is true, the heart may be right; "I do not understand Christ," says one, "but I will die for Him." Ignorance is no bar to salvation, and God will accept the humble worshipper. But He who made all things to the praise of His glory, made the mind as well as the heart, and will be worshipped with the understanding also. Therefore He has given His Holy Word, written, that men may know, and, understanding, love him. "God is a Spirit, and they that worship Him must worship Him in spirit and in truth."

We refrain—as our space will not permit—from any exhibition of Scripture proofs to sustain our positions. They who may wish to examine for themselves will find, in the works of Pearson, Leslie, and Jones alone, enough to satisfy them that the Church is deficient neither in Scripture nor argument, but is amply armed with both, for the maintenance of the doctrine of the holy, blessed, and glorious Trinity.

From the days when St. John contended with Cerinthus to the present time, the enemies of the faith have been instant in assailing the Church upon this vital point. They have ever failed in their fell design. The Church, true to her sacred trust, firm and unshaken in the truth, has always most jealously and unwaveringly held fast this all-important doctrine, and never ceased to present it, as she now presents it, as the first principle of the true, Catholic faith. So doing, she has perfect assurance that God is with her.

Having stated the doctrine of the Three Persons of the Godhead, let us briefly examine their respective offices and relations.

First. The Father, in virtue of his office, is Supreme. No man hath seen him. The Israelites knew nothing of the Father. We know him because the Son who was in the bosom of the Father, He hath declared him. The Father created all things; but he created them *by* the Son. Without the Son was not anything made. The Father created, yet the spirit of life, the Holy Spirit, moved upon the face of the waters. It was the Holy Spirit, too, who would not always strive with man. In the Old Testament the Deity is referred to under different appellations which are sometimes used interchangeably. We will mention three which we conceive to be the most prominent. *Elohim—Jehovah—Rooach-Elohim.* Yet the declaration is express and constant, "HEAR O ISRAEL, THE LORD THY GOD, *is eloi echad*, ONE GOD, THE ONLY GOD." GOD, we may add, is derived from the Icelandic *Godi*—"Supreme Magistrate," which may be traced in its turn to the ancient language from which the Icelandic came. The Father's peculiar office is that of Creator. As God the Father, he is the ancient of days—Supreme.

Second. The eternal, only-begotten Son of God the Father, being begotten of the same substance or essence, is necessarily coeternal with the Father. There never was a time when the Son was not; for being of the same substance, the one substance—God—to assert that there could have been such a time, would be to say that there was a time when God was not. The Son, in virtue of his office as Son, is subordinate to the Father. "My Father," he says, "is greater than I," that is, in point of office. The filial subordination must not be lost sight of. Coleridge objected to the Nicene Creed that it was not orthodox, being deficient in this doctrine. The office of the Second Person of the Trinity prior to his incarnation may be summed up in the declaration, that, "by him all things were made," and that he was the Jehovah-Angel, the Lord, the God of Israel.

The identity of Jehovah and our Lord Jesus is sustained now upon very strong philological grounds. "Jehovah, the ineffable name of God," says a writer in the *Church Monthly* (February, 1861), "which the son of Abraham never utters, is composed of four consonants YHVH—J and Y being the same. Owing to Hebrew having been originally written without vowels, and the sound of the ineffable name never heard, the pronunciation of it became lost. About 500 A. D., the Masorites, supposed to have belonged to a school at Tiberias, invented and attached to the Hebrew text certain points to supply the place of vowels. As the YHVH was never pronounced, the Masorites placed under those consonants the vowel points of the word Adonai,—'*Lord*,'—the name which the Jews to this day employ in reading whenever the mysterious name occurs. Much discussion has arisen in regard to the pronunciation, derivation, and signification of YHVH, rendered, in the Anglican version of the Bible, Jehovah. For a long time it was supposed to contain simply the idea of self-existence. Ewald, however, the first Hebraist living, writes the word so that it will read YAHVEH, the future of the verb '*to.be*.' Hence it means '*I will be*,' and is synonymous with the I AM THAT I AM, literally, *I will be that I will be* (Ex. iii. 14), God's 'memorial to all generations.' Undoubtedly the YHVH contains in its root the ideas of pure existence and self-existence. In the future form it also includes the idea of futurity. Thus it is fully rendered in Revelation i. 8, 'I am Alpha and Omega, the Beginning and the Ending, which is and which was, and which *is to come*.' Elohim, the Adonai-Yehevih or Jehovah, and Joshua or Jesus, all centre in the *immanoo*-AIL (Isaiah vii. 14), 'GOD WITH US.'" Thus the identity is preserved from Genesis to Revelation.

After His incarnation, the Second Person took upon Himself in addition the office of Redeemer. To enlarge upon the latter would carry us far beyond our present limits. We need only say that the especial office of the Son now is that of the Saviour. To him we owe the hope of eternal Life, and as he has declared, so by him we come to the Father.

Third. The Holy Spirit appears on the threshold of creation. He also now maketh intercession for us, and is the medium of the special grace of God to the souls of men. His office is that of Inspirer, Comforter, Sanctifier. He dwells in the Church during the absence of her Lord and Head, and keeps and guides her in her path to Heaven.

Thus distributed throughout the Three Persons of the Trinity is the action of the Deity. Yet there is but one God, and all that is thought or done is thought and done by Him. As Sir Thomas Browne says, "He holds no counsel, but that mystical one of the Trinity, wherein, though there be Three Persons, there is but one mind, that decrees without contradiction." There is but one will—the Divine will. The Unity is one in the Trinity, and the Trinity is one in the Unity.

Such is the conception of God which we derive from Reason and Revelation. Reason tells us that there is a God, and that he must be Wisdom, Goodness, Power. Revelation is a development of God from God, and discovers to us just so much as He wills we should know. More we cannot attain to.

> "Canst thou by searching find out God?
> Canst thou find out the Almighty to perfection?
> Heights of heaven! what canst thou do?
> Deeper than hell! what canst thou know?"

We return, then, to our original premise—"Man cannot comprehend God." The finite cannot include the infinite. A self-existent, perfect Being, in whom time is no element, exceeds our understanding. He is not as we are. His ways are not as our ways. His thoughts are not as our thoughts.

> "With God is wisdom and power,
> Counsel and understanding are his."

This being the case,—it being of God's condescension that we know anything,—let us accept the declarations of Reason and Revelation. Instead of "arguing with God," let us adore his perfections, acknowledge his goodness, and obey his commands, assured that we shall one day "see Him as He is."

Praise Father, Son, and Holy Ghost.

JEHOVAH-EVE.

In the fourth chapter of Genesis, it is related that Eve, after the expulsion from Paradise, "bare Cain, and said, I have gotten a man from the Lord." The correctness of this translation has been long questioned. The Hebrew words *kanithi ish eth-Jehovah* literally mean, "I have gotten the man Jehovah." Dr. Jarvis, in his admirable work, "The Church of the Redeemed," strongly defends this rendering, and quotes Parkhurst in support of it. The latter says: "It is a certain rule, that where *two* nouns, with *eth* between them, immediately follow a verb, the latter is in apposition with, or relates to, the same subject as the former, especially if the latter noun be a proper name." Luther, also, in his latest editions, maintains a similar rendering of the above passage. We would add that the word *ish*, "man," is without the article; hence it is defined by the word which follows in apposition, rendered emphatic by the particle *eth*. Thus, by some, *eth* is considered to be equivalent to "even":—"I have gotten a man, *even* Jehovah." But the first rendering is, in our judgment, more nearly accurate, and equally meets the requirements of exegesis.

The speech or exclamation of Eve is a sequence of the name *Cain*, "a possession," and explains what that "possession" was, viz., the man Jehovah. To comprehend the force of it fully, it is necessary to understand the meaning of the word Jehovah. This we will endeavor briefly to explain.

The mysterious name, the Ham-sem-pho-rash, or ineffable name of God, which the son of Abraham never utters, is composed of the four consonants YHVH,—J and Y being the same. Owing to Hebrew having been, like all Oriental languages, originally written without vowels, and the sound of the ineffable name never heard, the true pronunciation of it became lost, even among the Jews. About 500 A. D., the earliest Masorites, supposed by R. Sevita to have belonged to a school at Tiberias, invented and attached to the Hebrew text certain points, to supply the place of vowels. As the YHVH was never pronounced, the Masorites placed under those consonants the vowel points of the word Adonai, "LORD,"—the name which the Jews to this day employ in reading whenever the mysterious name occurs. As a natural consequence, much discussion has arisen not only in regard to the pronunciation, but to the derivation and signification of the YHVH, translated in the Anglican version of the Bible JEHOVAH. For a long time it was supposed to contain simply the idea of being—self-existence. But Bunsen, in his "Bibel-Werk," declares that Jehovah is no word at all,—consequently a manufacture,—and renders it by *Der Ewige*, "The Eternal."* Ewald, however, doubtless the first Hebraist living, the successor of Eichhorn and Michaelis at Göttingen, condemns Bunsen's translation as not including the idea of *Selbständigkeit*, self-existence. Ewald derives the word from *hayah*, the pre-Masorite, ancient form of *havah*, "to be," and points it so that it will read YAHVEH, the future of the verb *to be*.† Hence it means "*I will be*," and is synonymous with the declaration I AM THAT I AM, literally, "*I will be that I will be*" (Exodus iii. 14, 15), God's "memorial to all nations." Gesenius, in the latest edition of his Lexicon, acknowledges that the word heretofore pointed *Jehovah* should be pointed *Yahveh*. Other distinguished Hebraists in Germany,

* Carey, also, in his "Translation of the Book of Job," renders Jehovah "The Eternal." But his reasons for doing so are quite unsatisfactory.

† *Hayah* doubtless became *havah* through "Aremaic influence." The Arabic correspondent, at this day, is *havay*. Most probably, *hayah* is not only the pre-Masorite, but the pre-Mosaic form of the verb. (See EWALD'S *Hist. of the Children of Israel*, vol. ii., p. 204.)

The Hebrew language has, as is well known, but TWO tenses—the *perfect* and the *imperfect*. The primary meanings of these tenses are those of "*completeness*" and "*incompleteness*," involving the ideas of "*past*, *present*, and *future*." But the imperfect tense certainly contains the idea of our English future, and being often thus rendered, is by some styled the future tense. We are inclined to the opinion that the tense in question is so legitimately rendered in the present case, relating, as it does, to the Great Being, "who was, and is, and is to come,—the same yesterday, to-day, and forever."

we learn from Professor Hawkes, of Trinity College, Hartford, for some time a pupil of Ewald at Göttingen, also concur in the new pointing of the YHVH. Fürst, however, while he admits that the word is derived from *havah*, says that it should properly be pointed *Yeheveh*, in accordance with the *eheyeh*, etc. of Exodus iii. 14. That it is wrongly pointed now *Jehovah* with the vowels of *Adonai*, is admitted by all. The difference between the pointing of Ewald and that of Fürst would not materially vary the signification of this mysterious word; which indeed is the important question, and the one that we proposed to explain. Undoubtedly the YHVH contains in its root the ideas of *Sein* and *Selbständigkeit*, of pure existence and self-existence. In the future form, as pointed by Ewald, it also includes the idea of futurity. Thus it is fully rendered in Revelations i. 8, "I am Alpha and Omega, the Beginning and the Ending, which is, and which was, and which *is to come*,"—not only *o esomenos*, but *o erchomenos*.

Elohim, the name of the Creator in the first chapter of Genesis, composed of *Ail*, "almighty," in the plural form, and the *heth* of the *havah*, "to be,"—the *Adonai-Yehevih* of Abraham, Gen. xv. 2, 8,—and the *Jesus* of the New Testament, all centre in the *immanoo*-Ail (Isaiah vii. 14), "God with us,"—the Jehovah or Yahveh-Christ.

Jah or *Yah* is the component of many Hebrew names, as: *Jehoash*, "the fire of the Lord"; *Jehoiada*, "the knowledge of the Lord." *Joshua*, spelt in the

Law and the Prophets *Yehoshua*, and in the Hagiographa *Yaishua*, is composed of *Yah* and *Yasha*, "to save." It is thought by some that Joshua's original name was *Hoseah*, "Saviour," and that Moses added *Yah* to it after the defeat of the Amalekites, or even later (writers are not agreed in regard to the time). Joshua is precisely the same as the Greek Jesus, which is interpreted by Philo to be the "salvation of the Lord,"—the word Lord being *Kurios* in the Septuagint and New Testament, and *Yahveh* in the Hebrew.

It is worthy of note that the latest investigations of Mr. Layard at Nineveh, and of Sir Henry Rawlinson in Mesopotamia, decidedly confirm the elucidation we have given of the YHVH. The name Yav,—one of the oldest of the Assyrian deities, the god of the air,—which is unquestionably synonymous with the Hebrew *Yah* or *Yahveh*, has been clearly identified upon the cylinders found at Ur of the Chaldees, Abraham's birthplace. It is also thought to form an element in the name of a son of the king of Ur. The verification is singular and interesting, showing that there is no Scripture truth which is not strengthened by investigation.

The views above given of the identity of the God of Israel and our Saviour are not new. They have ever existed in the Church, and lain at the foundation of her theology,—the theology of the Bible, and not of man. Our readers will find the question referred to fully set forth in "Pearson on the Creed," especially in a note to the second article. It was also well presented a few years since in a popular form, by Mr. Alex. McWhorter, in a small volume entitled the "Memorial Name." * We are indebted to him for much of our information.

But to return to Eve. Our first mother did not know her Creator by any other name than that of Elohim. She never spoke of Him by any other name. She did not know that Yahveh was the name of God, or that God was to be her Redeemer. She only knew that the promise,—"I will put enmity between thee and the woman, and between thy Seed and her Seed: it shall bruise thy head and thou shalt bruise his heel," (Gen. iii. 15),—had gone forth. She believed that she would be avenged of the serpent; and when Cain was born, she joyfully hailed him as the promised "seed" who would

"Restore her and regain the blissful seat,"

from which Elohim had driven her in punishment for the transgression of His command. No wonder then that she regarded him as a "possession" of great price, and that she exclaimed with exultation, "I have gotten the man Yahveh."

Not long after—how long is not recorded—Eve gave birth to another son and called him Abel, "vanity," or "emptiness." She did not select this name

* Since this was written Mr. McWhorter has taken orders in the Church, and has republished the book above alluded to. It should be read by all who have examined Colenso's Second Part. "It is," says Dr. Williamson, of Toronto, "the only fundamental reply to the bishop's Part II. that has yet appeared, striking the whole ground from under him, by grappling with the central point on which he rests his case."

from any want of maternal feeling, but from contrasting him in her mind with his brother, in whom all her hopes were centred, and in whom she believed the promise to be bound up. It is recorded by Haggai that the second Temple, "in the eyes of those who had seen the house in her first glory, was in comparison as nothing." Such was Abel in the eyes of his mother; he was as nothing in comparison with the Seed who should "bruise the serpent's head."

We need not describe how the hopes of Eve were blasted, or how deep was her misery and mortification when she discovered that Cain was not the Deliverer, but the one who, by the murder of his brother, brought home to her heart the most fearful realization of the effects of that sin which her disobedience had introduced into the world. "Alas now for Eve!" says Mr. Melvill, "harboring a thought that God would not carry His threatenings into execution." Cain, her "possession," was a "fugitive," and Abel had too sadly verified his name.

At the birth of Seth, which occurred some time later, Eve appears to have been comforted; for the name indicates that she felt Elohim had not forsaken her. He was still her guardian. God "abideth faithful."

The history of Eve terminates here. In connection with the name Jehovah, however, there is one more passage in the chapter referred to, which deserves notice, and to which we will briefly allude before taking leave of the subject.

In the last verse it is said, that after Enos was born, "then began men to call upon the name of the Lord," or, as the author of the "Memorial Name" renders the passage, "to invoke with the name Yahveh." Then men who had heretofore only known God by the name of Elohim, became fully cognizant of His peculiar name, and invoked Him and adored Him by the name Jehovah or Yahveh. We have not space to go into an analysis of the contents, but we are confident that, upon an examination of the Hebrew, they will be found to corroborate the above translation and interpretation of the passage in question. It is due to the author of the "Memorial Name" to say, that among the many who have attempted to elucidate this difficult passage, he is the first who has really thrown any light upon it; and we must add that he has made what was heretofore dark perfectly clear and comprehensible. This is a good service,—one which the Biblical exegesis will appreciate. It is also another confirmation of a principle which cannot be too clearly comprehended or too often enforced, that the thread of Scripture is the development of Christ. Our Saviour, on the way to Emmaus, beginning with Moses, interpreted all things concerning Jesus of Nazareth. The whole Bible is one concurrent testimony to Him. "Let no one,"—therefore, as St. Cyril enjoins,—"let no one separate the Old Testament from the New."

THE PERSONS OF ADAM AND JESUS.

ADAM, as the first man, was the head of humanity. Coming fresh from the hands of God, unsullied in thought, untainted by act, at unity with himself, and in harmony with his Maker, he must have been, in form and aspect as well as in moral and intellectual conformation, a model of perfection. We read that he was made in the "image of God." This expression refers, we apprehend, not only to the internal image which Adam possessed ere he was deformed by sin, but to the human body which, it was ordained before the foundation of the world, the Son of God should in the fulness of time assume. Thus Adam was the type of humanity, Christ the antitype; the image was in Heaven. The three agree.

But we seek in vain for any elucidation of the peculiar external characteristics of the first man. Comprehending in himself the entire *genus*, we cannot attribute to him the specialities of any one of the various species which time has developed out of the original stock. He was the father of every species. In his veins flowed the "one blood," of which it pleased God to make all men. He was the type of all his descendants. Each one, therefore, of whatever nation, may be said to resemble him. Yet, *quantum mutatus ab illo* must each one be, if, as Dr. South writes, "Aristotle was but the rubbish of an Adam."

No portrait with pen or pencil remains to illustrate the first man. To do justice to the subject two would be necessary,—one of the unfallen, and one of the fallen Adam,—for we cannot but believe that his aspect must have undergone some change upon the entering in of sin and his alienation from his Maker. As we have nothing to guide us, all speculations are absolutely futile. We will, therefore, neither waste time by recounting those which curious writers have indulged in, nor by adding any crude ones of our own; but, leaving the first man, we come to the Second.

As Adam was the head of created, so Christ is the Head of recreated man. The former in his unfallen state was but a man; the latter was not only a man, and free from sin, but in Him also "dwelt the fulness of the Godhead bodily." One was the man, the other the God-man. If, therefore, we may justly predicate external perfection of the first man, *à fortiori*, we cannot do less of the Second. Is it possible, under the circumstances, that the one may have nearly resembled the other? We think not; for, as we have already observed, Adam was the type of his descendants, while

Christ, though of two races, was, in his distinctive traits, undoubtedly a Jew. Our Saviour's particular humanity began after nearly four thousand years had produced various divergences from the type which was "very good," and was, of course, affected by such divergences. Our Lord, like all men, was descended from Adam; but, counting from the Deluge, he was descended from Shem and Ham. "In the course of His progenitors in the flesh, it is remarkable," says Dr. Jarvis, "that what the world would regard as a taint in human blood occurred at least four times. Ruth, the mother of Obed, David's grandfather, sprang from the incestuous race of Lot; Pharez was the son of Judah by his widowed daughter-in-law; Rahab, the wife of Salmon, was of the race of Canaan, with whom all intermarriages were forbidden, and who, if a hostess, was, from her occupation, at least of suspected fame; and Bathsheba, whatever may have been her subsequent life and character, was guilty of an ignominious crime, for which she was punishable with death. Divine Providence, perhaps, allowed these blemishes in the Messiah's human descent, to show that no other immaculate conception was necessary but that of Him who was not born of the will of the flesh, but was conceived of the Holy Ghost in the womb of a pure virgin." It is worthy of note, also, that the Japhetic race which prides itself upon its distinction was not represented, after the flesh, in Christ. But "God hath enlarged Japheth, and he hath dwelt in the tents of Shem."

The Jehovah-Elohim of Shem is the God of Japheth—the Redeemer of the children of Adam.

Seeing that we are unable to give any transcript of the form and features of the first man, how stands the question in regard to the Second? Are we any better informed with respect to him? The Gospels give no description of the personal appearance of Christ. For all that we know on the subject we are indebted exclusively to tradition. As the latter, however, is interesting, and may embrace a measure of truth, we will briefly exhibit it to our readers.

Publius Lentulus, assumed by some to have been proconsul of Judæa prior to Herod, is reported to have seen the Saviour, and to have written the following letter to the Roman Senate: "At this time appeared a man who is still living and endowed with mighty power; his name is Jesus Christ. His disciples call him the Son of God; others regard him as a powerful prophet. He raises the dead to life, and heals the sick of every description of infirmity and disease. This man is of lofty stature, and well proportioned; his countenance severe and virtuous, so that he inspires beholders with feelings both of fear and love. The hair of his head is of the color of wine, and from the top of the head to the ears, straight and without radiance, but it descends from the ears to the shoulders in shining curls. From the shoulders the hair flows down the back, divided into two portions, after the manner of the Nazarenes; his forehead is clear and without wrinkle; his face free from blemish, and slightly tinged with red; his physiognomy noble and gracious. The nose and mouth are faultless. His beard is abundant, the same color as the hair, and forked. His eyes are blue, and very brilliant. In reproving or censuring, he is awe-inspiring; in exhorting and teaching, his speech is gentle and caressing. His countenance is marvellous in seriousness and grace. He has never once been seen to laugh; but many have seen him weep. He is slender in person, his hands are straight and long, his arms beautiful. Grave and solemn in his discourse, his language is simple and quiet. In appearance he is the most beautiful of the children of men."

"The above portrait, apocryphal though it be, is at least one of the first upon record; it dates from the earliest period of the Church, and has been mentioned by most ancient fathers." Undoubtedly it came from the same source as that delineation of the Saviour which originated, and was not infrequent, in the Eastern Church. "In the primitive ages," writes Lord Lindsay, in reference to the Western Church, "the Saviour was represented, not personally, but as the genius of Christianity—a youthful form and figure, without any special likeness. The traditional head with which Europe is familiar, was unknown in the West till the fourth century, when the original was sent to Constantia, sister of the Emperor, by Eusebius, Bishop of Cæsarea, to whom she had written her request to that effect. It is, therefore, indisputably to the Greek

Church that we owe that most expressive type which, if not the actual likeness of the Redeemer, comes nearer our dreams of what that likeness may have been—never the ideal of Incarnate Deity—than Christian humanity could have hoped to soar." Constantine, it is said, caused many copies to be made of the head of Christ. Doubtless they were taken from the picture which his sister received from the Bishop of Cæsarea. Harmonizing as the traditional types of the Saviour do with the description contained in the letter of Lentulus, and agreeing generally with each other, we cannot doubt that there was a common source for all. We would account for the matter thus. It is reasonable to suppose that there must have been current in Palestine, during the greater part of the first century, descriptions of the form and features of Jesus, some of which were probably preserved in writing; precisely as there were in circulation among the Hebrew Christians, prior to the publication of the four Gospels, little evangels or "declarations," as St. Luke terms them in the proem to his Gospel. All such descriptions proceeded primarily from eye-witnesses, and doubtless agreed substantially. To them might be traced, we believe—were all records not effaced—not only the apocryphal letter we have quoted, and perhaps others of a similar character, but those portraits of the Saviour which were rife in the Eastern Church,—which, by their attractiveness and supposed fidelity, gradually obtained acceptance through out Christendom, and were rendered permanent by the genius of Christian art. We believe, also, that the traditional type of Christ, as seen in the works of the great masters, and elaborated in the letter of Lentulus, contains a large share of truth; and we cannot but rejoice that the Church has had preserved to her so eminently beautiful a representation of the appearance of her Lord and Master when on the earth.

It is unnecessary to add further description of our Lord's person. We have given the earliest, and, of course, the best. The relations given by John Damascenus in the eighth, and St. Anschaire and Nicephorus in the ninth century, are merely modified reproductions of the old tradition. Nicephorus maintains that St. Luke painted portraits of Jesus, the Twelve, and the Virgin, and that thus their likenesses have been preserved to us. This is too improbable to need refutation on our part. Both Damascenus and Nicephorus, we ought to say, assume that there was a marked resemblance between the Virgin and her divine Son. We will copy the description of the latter, that our readers may compare it for themselves with the letter of Lentulus. It will be remembered that the two were written eight centuries apart.

"It is certain there has always been a particular tradition in the Church concerning the figure and stature of our Saviour and his Apostles. I will here describe our Lord's person after the images which are believed to have been painted by St. Luke. He was very beautiful in the face, and about seven spithamas (six feet) high; his hair was inclining to be very fair, not thick, but a little curled; his eyebrows were black, and did not form exactly a semicircle. His eyes were large, lively, and something yellowish; his nose long, his beard black, and pretty short; but he wore his hair long; for the scissors had never been used upon his head, nor had the hand of any one touched him besides that of his mother the Virgin, when he was as yet a child. His neck was not stiff, nor his carriage lofty or proud. He stooped a little with his head; his complexion was almost the color of wheat; his countenance neither round nor sharp, but, like his mother's, something longish, and pretty much upon the vermilion. Gravity, prudence, meekness, and clemency, were painted in his face; in a word, he perfectly resembled his divine mother."

There are evident discrepancies, especially in regard to the color of the beard and eyes, between this description, the letter of Lentulus, and the traditional portraits of the Saviour. The latter appear to have been influenced by the spirit of antique beauty, the poetry of art; the former by the undeniable fact that Christ was a Hebrew. Which comes nearer the truth, we will leave our readers to judge. The general characteristics in these and in all the descriptions of the human person of our Lord that have come under our observation we conceive to be the same. It will be remembered that a measure of truth is all that we have claimed for the earliest and, perhaps, the best of them. No actual likeness, but only a general conception, of the aspect of the Son of Man, has been handed down to us; and, such as it is, we receive it with satisfaction. Variations in the delineations of Christ may be traced in the pictures of the middle ages; but as we are not writing from the standpoint of the artist, it is unnecessary to pursue the investigation further.

We cannot leave the subject without noticing one singular tradition which was prevalent at an early day concerning our Saviour's person. It is this: There was a report current among some of the primitive Christians, that Jesus, so far from possessing dignity and beauty of aspect, was mean in stature and ill-favored in countenance. Justin Martyr, Tertullian, and Clement of Alexandria, maintain the opinion with their usual force. Origen wavers, inclining both ways; while Celsus, the physician who flourished in the time of Tiberius, "in the true spirit of Grecian art and philosophy," says Dean Milman, "denies that the Deity could dwell in a mean form or in a low stature." The impression we have referred to, arose from a literal rendering of the following passages of the Prophet Isaiah:—

"As many were astonished at thee; his visage was so marred more than any man, and his form more than the sons of men." Is. lii. 14.

"He hath no form nor comeliness; and when we shall see him, there is no beauty that we should desire him. He is despised and rejected of men." Is. liii. 2.

If St. Peter's rule of exegesis is correct—"No

prophecy of Scripture is of any private (i. e. *separate*, according to Bishop Horseley) interpretation,"—we have only to collate the above passages with other portions of Holy Writ to perceive that a Procrustean literalism is quite inadmissible. For instance:—

Isaiah says: "In that day the Branch (of Zech. iii. 8, and Jer. xxiii. 5) of the Lord shall be beautiful and glorious." Is. iv. 2.

Zechariah exclaims: "How great is his beauty!" Zech. ix. 17.

The Psalmist, in more than one place, praises the "beauty of the Lord," and affirms: "Thou art fairer than the children of men." Psalms xxvii. 17; xlv. 2.

Moses, too, in one of his prayers, refers to "the beauty of the Lord." Psalm xc. 17.

Finally, Solomon, chanting the praises of the "Beloved" in his sublime lyric, declares, that "He is the chiefest among ten thousand, and altogether lovely." Cant. v. 10, 16.

Need we say more in refutation? Toward the close of the fourth century, when the spirit of poetry began to exhibit itself in the Church, and the influence of Christian art to be felt, the dishonoring impression relative to our Saviour's person appears, to a great extent, to have worn away. "Jerome, Chrysostom, Ambrose, and Augustine, with one voice," says Milman, "assert the majesty and engaging appearance of Christ." Chrysostom affirms that "the Heavenly Father forced upon him in full streams that corporeal grace which is distilled drop by drop upon mortal man;" and Augustine declares "that He was beautiful on his mother's bosom, beautiful in the arms of his parents, beautiful upon the cross, beautiful in the sepulchre." Still later some of the Fathers, such as Basil and Cyril, reproduced the old story of the meanness of the Redeemer's form and countenance; but this, we are led to think, arose from an ill-considered desire to exalt the moral beauty of Christ by contrasting it with unseemliness of person. However, all that is changed; truth has prevailed, we believe, and Augustine has triumphed over Cyril.

We have briefly discussed the question of the respective form and features, the appearance of the first and the second Adam. Concerning the former, we are obliged to admit that we know nothing, except that, like the residue of God's creation, he was "very good." That phrase, under the circumstances, surely intimates perfection. We may fairly assume, therefore, that in—

> "Adam, the goodliest man of men since born—
> Godlike, erect, with native honor clad—
> The image of his glorious Maker shone."

The Apollo, were it instinct with life and untainted by sin, would furnish but a feeble conception of the unfallen Adam. In the sight of God he was *very good.*

Of the latter or second Adam, we may say that St. Luke permits us to infer that, in childhood, he was gracious and attractive; prophecy speaks of him as wonderful and beautiful; and tradition, which we deem to be to some extent truthful, accounts him to have excelled the children of men in majesty, in grace, and in nobleness of mien. It would be strange, indeed, when the form that was made after the likeness of God was very good, if the form in which it pleased God to enshrine himself, should be deficient in dignity and grace. No, if the face is an index of character, if the outer man is expressive of the inner, the beauty in Jesus which could not be hidden, must have been adorned with outward grace, and rendered effective in an eminent degree by every attribute of human beauty commensurate with truth. "Assuredly," says St. Jerome, "the splendor and majesty of the hidden divinity shone even in his human countenance."

It should be ever remembered by all Christians, that the form which the eternal Son of God took when he was born into the world and joined the human nature to the divine, he assumed neither in appearance merely, nor temporarily, as was the case when, as the Jehovah-Angel, he appeared to Abraham at the "tent door" (Gen. xviii.), came to meet Joshua as "captain of the host of Israel" (Josh. v. 13), or "did wondrously" in the presence of Manoah (Judg. xiii.), but he took it forever. This was, this is, a part of his ineffable condescension. This, too, is what raises the human above the angelic nature, and places it at the pinnacle of creation. The form which the Son in his humiliation assumed, he redeemed and carried with him when he ascended to the right hand of the Majesty on high. He has it now; and in it he will return to reign and to judge, to be to each either the Christus Indemnificator or the Christus Consolator. Then we shall "see him as he is,"—we shall "see the King in his glory."

REDEMPTION.

THE doctrine of the Redemption involves the doctrines of the Incarnation and Atonement; indeed, we might say, all the doctrines of the Church. In approaching this important question, therefore, we are strongly reminded of the remark of an old clergyman whom a graduate from a theological seminary had requested to read his first sermon, desirous, of course, of profiting by the advice of his experienced friend. "Do you not intend," said the old gentleman, after kindly perusing the well-studied discourse, "to write any more sermons?" "Certainly," replied the young clergyman, "I hope to write many more. Why do you ask the question?" "I observed," quietly responded the other, "that you had put the whole of the Christian religion in this one, and it occurred to me that, perhaps, you might not intend to write any more." We assure our readers that we have no designs upon their patience. We do not propose to assume, in the language of a distinguished bishop, "that the majority of a Christian community do not know what Christianity is "—an assertion which is not less true than sad—for the purpose of opening the way for the evolution of the whole subject in a single essay. We rather intend to follow the example of the orator who divided his subject into one hundred parts, and then dispensed with ninety-nine of them—that is, thoroughly appreciating the active power of a principle when duly lodged in the mind, he omitted a great deal of mere verbiage, and confined himself to the leading idea which he wished to enforce. In like manner we shall endeavor to present a concise view of the distinctive doctrine of Christianity. We say distinctive, because Christianity is a scheme of Redemption.

We have often heard it asserted that the essence of the Gospel, the peculiar excellence of the Christian religion, consists in the noble precepts laid down in the Sermon on the Mount. Thus they would condense Christianity into one sentence, viz: "Whatsoever ye would that man should do unto you, do ye so even unto him." Now, Confucius uttered almost identically the same sentiment five hundred and fifty years before Christ; and Socrates enunciated precepts, such as "forgiveness of injuries," quite in accordance with those delivered in the sermon referred to. Many heathens and infidels, too, have obeyed the laws, and exhibited a temperance, self-denial, and kindness of feeling that would compare favorably with those virtues as displayed by acknowledged Christians. There must be something else, then, that differences the Christian religion from every other. Judaism contained Christianity. If it had any vitality, it derived it from Christ. The law, we know, was merely a "pedagogue." We therefore pass over Judaism in our examination. All other religions of which we have any account, comprehend a *cultus*, or worship, and a moral life. The measure of each depends upon the character of the religion. Only Christianity teaches that man is purchased with a price; that he must love his fellow-man because God has loved him; that he must forgive his fellow-man because God hath forgiven him. Only Christianity teaches that man, created in the image of God in Adam, must be recreated in the image of God in Christ. What distinguishes the Christian religion, then, from every other, is that it is the religion of Christ. The mode is Redemption; the end is Sanctification; the formula is the Church. Man is out of Christ; the Church is the instrument by which he may be in Christ and Christ in him.

But to return to the doctrine of the Redemption in particular. We have said that it involves those of the Incarnation and Atonement. The truth of this assertion will become apparent as we proceed. We will, therefore, consider the two doctrines in their natural order.

We premise that there are four natures of which we are cognizant. One, uncreate, self-existent, infinite, eternal—God; one, created, spiritual, immortal—*Angels;* one, created, finite, immortal—*Man;* one, created, indifferent, mortal—*Animals*. Of the first we need not speak here. Of the second we will not speak, as it is aside from our subject, and we would avoid any curious speculation. The third comprises in its entirety an immortal spirit (*pneuma*), an animal soul (*psyche*), and a material body (*sarx kai aima*)—*geist*, *seele*, *und leib*. The fourth possesses an animal soul and a material body more or less inferior to that of the second. It is indifferent, having no moral quality, and is completely mortal.

What differences, in the highest degree, the human from the animal nature, is the immortal spirit which informs the former and renders it accountable. For instance, man reasons; so does the animal, though in a lower degree. Man has instinct; so has the animal, and in a higher degree. Man remembers and recollects. The animal remembers, but cannot recollect. Man's nature is positive; his acts have a moral quality; they must be relatively either good or bad. The animal nature is indifferent; its acts are neither good nor bad; they are natural. Man is a living spirit, an accountable being, made in the image of God, immortal. The animal is a creature merely, unaccountable, made to perish, mortal. The one will ascend to God; the other will bow down in the dust forever.

What differences the human from the angelic nature is, that though man's body was made of the dust of the earth and must thither return, his nature, through Christ, has been brought into contact with the Divine nature, and thus ennobled. The extremes of position which the human nature occupies are wonderful. "With what little humiliation," exclaims Pascal, "the Christian compares himself with the worm of the earth! with what little pride he believes himself united to God!"

The human nature was created last. On the sixth Mosaic day God created Adam. In him dwelt the whole human nature. Subsequently it was varied and enlarged in its presentation by Eve being taken out of Adam. She was not created *like* Adam, or *as* Adam, but *in* Adam. Hence Eve was as much the child of Adam as Seth, Solomon, or Salome.

The nature of Adam and Eve was originally upright. Their wills were in accordance with the will of God. They knew no sin. Tempted, however, by Satan, they transgressed and fell from their pure estate. Their wills became, in consequence, diverse from the will of God, and their tendency evil continually. The nature which was all in Adam necessarily descended in its entirety to his posterity. Precisely as the episcopate which was all in Christ, descended all to the Apostles, and from them to their successors. The episcopate is one. Human nature is one in the same sense.

A fearful result of the disobedience of Adam was, that he and his descendants, who must inherit the fallen nature, became amenable to the punishment of death, —not physical death, for that was in the world before sin entered, and was not a consequence of sin,—but spiritual death—the everlasting punishment, in some form, of man hereafter. In comparison with the latter or "second death," physical death sinks into insignificance. "The death of the body is not reckoned," says Alford, "as death any more than the life of the body is life in our Lord's discourses. Physical death is overlooked and disregarded in the New Testament in comparison with that which is really death." Besides, to fallen man, physical death, like labor, is a blessing. It is not really death, but the beginning of life indeed. "For a Christian to be amazed at death," says Sir Thomas Browne, "I see not how he can escape this dilemma—that he is too sensible of this life, or hopeless of the life to come."

The purposes of God, however, which are from everlasting—with him there is no variation—could not be frustrated by the machinations of Satan or the weakness of man. No sooner had the latter fallen than the promise of the Redeemer, the "Lamb slain from the foundation of the world," was published by the Almighty, and the way opened not merely for the restoration of man to his pristine state, but for his renovation and adaptation to a state of which that from which he fell was only a type. The Paradise of Christ will excel the Paradise of Adam as much as the second man excels the first.

We must not suppose, for a moment, that God failed in any way, that Satan or Adam compelled him to alter his way or vary his ultimate design. With the Almighty is perfection; his ways are eternal; his thoughts are equal; his plan is one. Creation, as has been finely said, was made for Redemption. Were it not so, there would be no place for Christ in the scheme of this world. Now we know that all God's purposes are in Christ. Hence Christ's Redemption is God's plan. Praise ye the Lord!

The first step in the Divine plan was the Incarnation. It took place thus. In the fulness of time, God the Father sent his only-begotten son, begotten of his own, one, substance, God with himself, to redeem mankind. By the power of the Holy Ghost a man-child was conceived in the womb of the Virgin Mary, whose nature was the same as that of any other virgin. To this child, in the womb, God the Son voluntarily joined himself; his will being the same with the will of Him who sent him. Thus the God-man was born into the world. The complete union of perfect God and perfect man, inseparable forever, formed one Christ. Our Saviour did not take upon himself the nature of Adam before the fall. Had he done that we should have no part in him. But he took upon himself the nature of Adam after the fall. Yet Christ knew no sin. The perfect union of the Divine and the human purged the latter from the sin incident to its fallen state. God and sin could not be one, and Christ is one. Moreover, God took the human nature into the Divine for the very purpose of cleansing the former. *Suscipit, et suscipit ut mundaret suscipiendo.* "He took it, and he took it that he might cleanse it in taking it," as St. Augustine observes.

Sanctification, or the cleansing, renovation, and exaltation of the human nature, began in the individual Jesus, and was perfected in him with respect to himself without regard to time. If we add that the exaltation was perfected legally at the Ascension, when Christ presented the human nature, having caused it to triumph over death, perfect, to God the Father, it will not alter the proposition, as the latter was the legal conclusion of the great transaction. But Sanctification with respect to the whole human nature was not perfected at once. The spiritual life, however, which it had lost in the fall, was restored. By God's condescension in becoming man, the human nature already tried and condemned, was brought into absolute contact with, and joined to the Divine nature. Thus the whole human nature by one act was raised from its abased, spiritually dead, insalvable state, reëndowed with life, and declared salvable. The character or tendency of human nature was not altered. It remained evil continually—that is, its inclination is to evil rather than good. But the *status* of the nature before God was changed. Whereas, it was dead and could not live, the germ of life was introduced into it, and man became really a "living spirit." Whereas, being dead, it was insalvable, being quickened, it became salvable. Further, the general grace granted to man through the elevation of his nature by the effect of the Incarnation enables man to listen to the voice of the Holy Spirit, to turn to God and seek salvation. The human nature was not only revived by the operation of the Incarnation, not only changed in regard to its legal *status* before God, but it was *enabled.*

Yet human nature was not renovated,—man was not absolutely saved by the Incarnation. To effect the renovation of human nature, which in its perfection is salvation, another step in the Divine plan became necessary, viz: a propitiation for sin. This brings us to the Atonement.

At the time appointed in the council of God—the mysterious Senate of the Trinity—the Lord Jesus Christ, who, by virtue of his Godhead, belonged to that Senate where there was but one will—the Divine will —and whose human will was in perfect accord with his Divine will, voluntarily submitted to be crucified, and thus became a ransom for the sins of man both original and actual.

The propitiation does not consist in Christ's sufferings being an equivalent for the sin of the whole world, which was indeed laid upon him, and thus the debt paid; nor, that through such suffering, the law violated by Adam and the unkept Mosaic law were vindicated, the sanction of physical death having been enforced at the expense of an innocent person voluntarily undergoing the penalty; for then man would not be liable to judgment. It consists in this, that man, being fallen, and it being certain that he will sin, and yet have nothing to offer to God whereby he may obtain forgiveness of sin, God, " who was in Christ reconciling the world unto himself," was pleased to make Himself, in the Person of his Son, an atonement for sin which man might plead at the bar of the Majesty on high, provided he should do so in faith, and thus obtain not only pardon, but reward. Thus man's responsibility is united to God's work, and man's moral agency is conserved. Thus, too, God's justice and holiness, which are inseparable, are maintained, His unspeakable love displayed, and His glory, to the praise of which all things in heaven and earth consist, is manifested throughout creation and Redemption, from everlasting to everlasting.

The action of the Atonement differs from that of the Incarnation, though both are parts of one scheme. In the latter there was an *opus operatum;* the volition was all on the part of God. Man had not, and could not have anything to do in it; he was the quiescent recipient through his common nature of the benefit. To profit by the Atonement, however, they to whom it is directly offered—that is, they to whom the Gospel is preached—must coöperate. They must have faith; for God has decreed, that, as man being concluded under sin can have no righteousness of his own, he will accept of faith in Christ in lieu thereof. Man is not *made* righteous, but the righteousness of Christ is imputed to him and he is *accounted* righteous for his faith. This righteousness, which theologians term " forensic," must not be confounded with the practical righteousness which flows from and is the evidence of a living faith. (Cf. Rom. v. 1, and Heb. xii. 11.) The first is Justification; the second is the beginning of Sanctification. "Without holiness no one shall see God."

Faith, it will be perceived, is of vital importance. The grace which flows from the Incarnation will inspire initial faith—that is, it is sufficient to do so—faith to arise and be baptized, and become a member of Christ and an heir through Him of salvation. It is each man's own fault if he rejects the proffered grace. In addition, God has promised to send his Holy Spirit to dwell not only in the Church during the absence of her Lord, but also in the heart of every one who shall not refuse him, to keep alive faith. Thus "by grace are ye saved through faith."

"Grieve not the Holy Spirit." For, as Doctor Trench shows, "the spiritual is superinduced on the natural, and grace does not dissolve the groundwork of individual character." Man remains man; his will is unfettered: he is a free agent; he can neglect or accept "such great salvation." Contemplate the two pictures. If he neglect it, he will surely die,—if he accept it, Christ, who has fulfilled the office of Redeemer, in exalting the human nature—of Prophet, in proclaiming the glad tidings—of Priest, in offering the sacrifice—of Victim, in being himself the "slain Beauty of Israel" —shall return to exercise the office of Judge Eternal— by the means of faith he will be enabled to plead the merits of Christ, and will receive, according to God's covenant, pardon and salvation. He no longer will be simply *accounted* righteous, but he will be *made* righteous. He will not be restored to Eden, the Paradise of Adam, but admitted to the New Jerusalem, the city of the Lamb. "It is not to restore the old," says Alford, "but to create the new, that Redemption has been brought about. Whatever may have been God's image in which the first Adam was created, it is certain that the image of God in which Christ's spirit recreates us will be as much more glorious than that as the second Man was more glorious than the first."

Such is the doctrine of Redemption, which the Church teaches as revealed in Holy Scripture; and to which her sacraments, prayers, and teachings are all subordinate. Christ is the Redeemer; the Church is the minister of Redemption to mankind. Happy are they who believe in God, confess the Lord Jesus, and listen to the voice of the Holy Spirit.

We forbear to pursue the subject further. When we reflect upon the mystery, the magnitude, and the mercy of the great plan of the Almighty which we have endeavored to unfold, our minds are filled with wonder and admiration; and we are tempted to exclaim with the Apostle: "O the depth of the riches both of the wisdom and knowledge of God! Who shall separate us from the love of Christ?"

GRACE.

Confessedly grace is a difficult subject. Perhaps no point in theology, save the doctrine of the Trinity and its correlates, has given rise to more discussion. This proceeds to some extent from the question interlacing itself with other important doctrines. The latter, also, adds to its complexity; for relative subjects always influence each other's solution. Thus an error with respect to grace surely repeats itself in other parts of that great scheme which is so permeated by this principle that in contradistinction to pure natural religion and the letter of the Mosaic dispensation, it is termed the scheme of grace. It must not be inferred, however, that grace, which is the antithesis of nature, as we shall hereafter more particularly show, was wanting in the Mosaic dispensation. Quite the contrary is the fact. But grace did not hold so conspicuous a place in the type as it does in the antitype, in the shadow as in the reality. Christ was hidden in the law, revealed in the Gospel.

All Christians must, from the necessity of the case, accept a doctrine of grace; yet much diversity of opinion exists in regard to the nature of grace, its process and effect. Admittedly the question is not easily defined. Nevertheless we will attempt the task; merely premising that our standpoint is that of the Church as declared by sincere, Protestant Church theologians. We will begin by separating our subject and putting it in a definite position, that it may be firmly seized and plainly examined.

Grace proper—we refer to it here in its theological acceptation, and not in any of the various senses in which the word is often used—falls naturally under three principal heads, viz.: 1. General Grace; 2. Sacramental Grace; 3. Particular Grace. We will treat our subject accordingly, and we hope thus with more clearness.

When God breathed into Adam the "breath of life" (literally *two* lives—the natural and the spiritual), He endowed him with a nature which we call "human." This nature Adam possessed entire in himself. By the instigation of Satan, through the disobedience of Adam, sin entered into the world and corrupted Adam's nature, so that it became guilty in the sight of God. Hence Adam individually and generically was condemned to death in accordance with the sanction attached to God's command: "Of the tree of the knowledge of good and evil thou shalt not eat; for in the day thou eatest thereof, thou shalt surely *die*." The death referred to was not physical death,—for that had ever been the correlative of animal life, and had in an especial manner marked the close of every one of the completed six formative eons known as Mosaic days,—but spiritual death; a death which began by the introduction of sin through the Devil, to be finally perfected in "everlasting destruction from the presence of the Lord." We care not to define it here more particularly. The heirs and descendants of Adam, from Eve down, necessarily inherited the corrupted or fallen nature; and thus all mankind, obvious to death, lay under the ban of heaven. Had they realized their position, verily might they have exclaimed: "Our punishment is greater than we can bear." But, as has been finely observed: "Man's extremity is God's opportunity." The Prophet Isaiah writes: "The Lord saw that there was no man, and wondered that there was no intercessor; therefore His arm brought salvation unto him; and His righteousness it sustained him." (Is. lix. 16.) When the Eternal Son, being God with the Father, was incarnate, He took the one human nature up into His own Divine nature, and so raised it from its state of condemnation to a position where it could, on God's terms, be saved. Thus, at one blow, God redeemed human nature from the ban which sin had brought upon it, and rendered it amenable to grace. Further, He endowed the nature with a grace which counteracts, in a measure, its debility, enables the nature beyond what itself was equal to. This grace operates upon the nature in aggregate, or constitutionally. It is what we call General Grace; it is the grace of our Lord Jesus Chriist.

But the Incarnation, although it changed the legal status of mankind by the work wrought upon the common nature, did not save man. Why? Because God, while in one respect He treats man as a whole—a race—in all others, He treats him as an individual, requiring from him individual character. God does not save man by an *opus operatum*, but offers to save, and will covenant to save him, if he will obey His commands. Neither is the grace which flows from the Incarnation, though it removes the torpidity of the nature, and enables man thus far, that he is a responsible being, accountable to Christ, sufficient in all respects for a nature which, though redeemed, is still fallen. Man, be it remembered, is "very far gone from original righteousness." Moreover, sin is death; salvation is life. Hence the necessity of an atonement to annul sin by the satisfaction of the law. The death of Christ was the correlative of His birth. To minister Himself and his atonement to man, our Saviour planted His Church and ordained His ministry. The work of the latter, however diverse or various it may be, heads up in that; that, finally, is its end and sum. In that Church, which we call *One*, because we never heard of any other; *Holy*, on account of Christ, its Head, the holiness incident thereto, and the holiness required of it; *Catholic* or *Universal* with regard to time, place, people, faith, and practice, and its Divine ministration of all the means of grace; *Apostolic*, having been built upon the foundation of the Apostles and Prophets, Jesus Christ being the chief corner-stone, and continuing steadfastly in the Apostle's doctrine and fellowship—in that Church so fitly framed, so nobly planned, so Divinely called, our Saviour instituted two eminent Sacraments, "the outward signs of inward and spiritual grace." By the first, man is baptized *into* Christ, and the life of Christ is grafted *into* him; this is the life by which he lives, having become a member of Christ's body, and entered into covenant with God. By the second, man obtains, if he partake rightly, spiritual food for the nourishment of the life which was grafted into him in baptism. The mutual operation of the two is manifest. The one demands the other, while both are direct mediums in the Church for the application of the atonement. Out of each of these Sacraments flows a grace to the due recipient; for Christ is acting in them; otherwise they would be but mere forms. The grace which is thus vouchsafed is something which God grants in addition to the life sacramentally born and nourished. It affords aid and comfort against the enemy, and succors man in his endeavor to profit by such distinguished means of grace. This grace we term Sacramental Grace; it is also the grace of our Lord Jesus Christ.

In addition, God also grants unto man individually further grace to meet every emergency, to act and to endure, to live and to die. It is seen in the prevenient grace which prompts man to repent, to seek Christ, and to enter into covenant relation with God. It is seen in the "heavenly grace" incident to the Apostolic rite of Confirmation. It is seen in the grace which converts the heart,—a conversion which every adult soul requires; for the Church is not, as the Romanist in fact maintains, a great mechanical Sacrament, which saves *per se*,— and it is seen in the "grace to help in time of need" of which every one must feel the want, and by which alone can man run well, or hopefully, the race that is set before him. "We have no power," says Article X., "to do good works pleasant and acceptable to God, without the grace of God by Christ preventing us, that we may have a good will, and working with us, when we have that good will." This is what we call Particular Grace; it is "*by* Christ," as all grace is by Christ, but it is especially the Fellowship of the Holy Ghost.

Although we have thus classified grace, and it appears not less varied than multiplied in its manifestation, let it not be supposed that grace is deficient in unity. It is all one even as He is one. Creation, Redemption, Sanctification, are all God's act, parts of one great whole, though their execution brings out, and before us, the three Divine Persons of the Godhead. It concerns not how grace comes; it is all God's grace which emanates from His love. God's love in all its plenitude of grace and power streams out to man, whence, having performed its office, it returns to its Fountain, bringing with it the love of God.

God's grace must not be confounded with His mercy, nor thought an evasion of justice. "The word *grace* is often found," says Dean Trench, *Syn.* xlvii., "associated with *mercy*, (1 Tim. i. 2; 2 Tim. i. 2; Tit. i. 4; 2 Jno. 3). But, though standing in closest inner as well as outer connection, there is this difference between them, that *grace* has reference to the *sins* of men, *mercy* (compassion here) to their *misery*. God's free grace is extended to men as they are guilty, His compassion is extended to them as they are miserable. The lower creation may be, and is, the object of God's *compassion*, inasmuch as the burden of man's curse has redounded also upon it (Job. xxxviii. 41; Ps. cxlvii. 9; Jonah iv. 11), but of His grace man alone; he only needs, he only is capable of receiving it. In the Divine mind, and in the order of our salvation as conceived therein, the *compassion* precedes the *grace*. God so loved the world with a pitying love (herein was the mercy—compassion) that He gave His only begotten Son (herein the grace) that the world through Him might be saved; cf. Eph. ii. 4; Luke i. 78, 79. But in the order of the manifestation of God's purposes of salvation the grace must go before the mercy. It is true that the same persons are the subjects of both, being at once the guilty and the miserable; yet the righteousness of God, which it is just as necessary should be maintained as his love, demands that the guilt should be done away before the misery can be assuaged; only the forgiven can, or indeed may, be made happy; whom He has pardoned, He heals; men are justified before they are sanctified. Thus in each of the Apostolic salutations it is first grace, and then mercy which the Apostle desires for the faithful (Rom. i. 7; 1 Cor. i. 3; 2 Cor. i. 2; Gal. i. 3; Eph. i. 2; Phil. i. 2); nor could the order of the words be reversed." We will only add that mercy before grace is *anglice*, compassion; mercy after grace, clemency.

Two questions naturally arise out of our subject, viz.:—1. How does Grace operate? 2. Is it resistible?

The first question suggests the oft-repeated query, How does Inspiration act?—We must admit that we can no more define precisely how Grace operates than how Inspiration acts. The Spirit of God bloweth where it listeth. From what we know, however, of God and of man's spiritual and moral organization, we may assume that grace is a power of God,—that it operates upon man's spiritual or higher nature both as an influence and as a force; beginning, doubtless, as the former, and arising as received to the latter. General Grace, as we have described it, affects human nature in the aggregate—individuals generally; Sacramental Grace, every regenerate soul that duly partakes of the sacraments; Particular Grace, each individual, according to the purpose of God. Grace operates, we repeat, upon man's higher nature. Thus it may energize faith, awaken conscience, kindle love, or warm the heart. It is not, like faith, one of the powers of man's spiritual nature, but it is a power shed out by God through the second and third persons of his Deity upon one or all of the powers of the spiritual nature of man. Its highest office with respect to fallen man we deem to be that of arousing and maintaining in activity, faith. "By grace are ye saved through faith." Grace must precede faith, must energize faith; the latter will produce belief, action—a proper use of the means of grace which leads to the being in a state of grace. Thus grace is both a cause and an effect,—a power of God and a state of godliness. Precisely how Grace operates, however, we confess we are unable to define or illustrate. The same, as we have before remarked, is true of Inspiration. But we need not be curious on these subjects. They belong to the mysteries of Deity; and by searching shall we "find out God."

Our second question,—Is Grace resistible?—is one that has entered into many a polemic field. Pelagius, in the early part of the fifth century, denying the fall of man, and averring his ability to walk uprightly of himself, took the extreme ground of rejecting the doctrine of grace altogether; considering the latter not only quite superfluous, but derogatory to the dignity of human nature. He was fiercely and successfully opposed by St. Augustine.* This heresy, like many

* Perhaps Pascal's finest letters are on the question of grace. His discussions of the *pouvoir prochaine—grace suffisante* and *grace efficace*—are inimitable.

others, has been reproduced in modern times by some who are "wise beyond what is written." It leavens all who, while they profess to believe, maintain under any phase *humanitarian* views, or glory in the present as a humanitarian age. To do without grace is to do without Christ. The aspect of such, however elevated their natural development, however refined their intellectual culture, however beautiful their apparent adornment, reminds us of the poet's description of departed Greece, of beauty revealed in death :—

> "So coldly sweet, so deadly fair,
> We start, for *soul* is wanting there."

In the sixteenth century Calvin, who is considered by many to be a theological descendant of St. Augustine, took ground to the utmost extent in reverse of Pelagius, and in accordance with his iron system asserted the irresistibility of grace. If the latter is not literally embraced in his fourth and fifth points, it certainly is the inevitable correlative of them. The Protestant Church, however, which does not get up human systems, but simply unfolds the tenets of the Scriptures without subjecting them to a Procrustean operation, affirms the necessity of grace, and, at the same time, that it may not impugn the freedom of the will, teaches its resistibility. Were it not so, man would not be a responsible being. He would be an automaton; and God would be directly responsible for the loss of every soul that finally shall be cast away. Now the rule of

God's providence is, that having constituted man a free and responsible being, and furnished him with a "way," He wills that he should endeavor to walk in that way. This God empowers and enables him to do, having freely redeemed human nature from the curse, furnished, without price, a satisfaction for all sin, and given man assurance not only of grace to begin a life of righteousness, but of grace to continue therein. Nevertheless man must coöperate with God. "We are laborers together with God," says the Apostle, "we as workers together with Him beseech you that ye receive not the grace of God in vain." Man must "walk with God" on earth if he would be "taken" to God in heaven. Yet, even so, no credit can inure to man; for "it is God that worketh in him both to will and to do." The work is begun by God *in* man, and carried on by God *through* man. Thus, the coöperation and responsibility of man being conserved, all is made to work to the glory of God the Father through the grace of our Lord Jesus Christ and the fellowship of the Holy Ghost. The necessity and the resistibility of grace, therefore, as maintained in the collects and articles of the Church, indeed, in her whole doctrine and practice, is not only plain but Scriptural. "Without me," says our Saviour, "you can do nothing;" and St. Paul adds, "grieve not the Holy Spirit."

We have said that grace affects the spiritual nature of man. It does so primarily. But the influence and force, unless effectually resisted, is felt throughout spirit, soul, and body. The healthful and harmonious action of the whole man which ensues is the fruit of grace; or as some term it, a state of grace. The degree of the latter will depend upon the measure of God's gifts in each case vouchsafed, and the measure of acceptance with which it meets. Good seed will not produce good fruit, or abundantly, without good culture. Besides, God does not waste His gifts; nor does He deem them unworthy either of appreciation or return.

> "Nature never lends
> The smallest scruple of her excellence,
> But like a thrifty goddess she determines
> Herself the glory of a creditor,
> Both thanks and use."

It is worthy of remembrance that grace, however it may be contemned by the self-righteous, is a felt need of every true believer,—the firmer the belief the more urgent the feeling,—and that while God, in accordance with His unerring wisdom, proportions the gift, it is one for which man should most earnestly and incessantly pray. Christian life is a struggle. St. Paul at one time sought naturally to avoid the conflict. He prayed that the "thorn" might be removed. But he received answer: "My grace is sufficient for thee." Man must fight the fight if he will gain the prize; he must run the race if he will win the crown. This fighting and running are only other names for man's coöperating with Christ and the Spirit of Grace. St. Paul, be it observed, did not complain of the answer, found no fault with the terms, but proceeded to act upon the information in such wise that he was enabled to assert that he did not "war after the flesh," and that he had "fought a good fight," for he knew "in whom he trusted." We commend the example of the noble Apostle to our readers, assuring them that if they will earnestly employ all the means of grace, they will always "find grace to help in time of need."

FAITH.

APART from the mysterious doctrines of the Church which relate immediately to the Nature and Persons of God, no doctrine holds a higher place—if one can be properly said to hold a higher place where "all are fitly joined together"—than faith. It is distinguished by this peculiarity: it is the *working* doctrine of Christianity. Faith cannot be held abstractly at all. It either works or is not. Under Christ it is the active principle of all true religion. Strange to say, we not unfrequently hear faith entirely subordinated to charity by well-meaning persons, because St. Paul has said in that most beautiful chapter, 1 Cor. xiii. 13, "Now abideth faith, hope, charity, these three; but the greatest of these is charity." A little reflection will show why the Apostle expressed himself in this manner without detracting in any way from a due estimation of faith. In the next world faith cannot exist, for it will be lost in sight; hope will find no place, for it will be swallowed up in reality; only charity can remain. In this world it is quite different, however. Here we walk by faith, and not by sight. If we so walk, hope must attend our steps,—charity will not be wanting. In reply to those who set charity above or in the place of faith, Coleridge says: "To myself, formerly, it appeared a mere dispute about words: but it is by no means of so harmless a character, for it tends to give a false direction to our thoughts, by diverting the conscience from the ruined and corrupted state in which we are without Christ. Sin is the disease. What is the remedy? Charity? Pshaw! Charity, in the large apostolic sense of the term, is the health, the state to be obtained by the use of the remedy, not the sovereign balm itself,—faith of grace,—faith in the God-manhood, the cross, the mediation, the perfected righteousness of Jesus, to the utter rejection and abjuration of any righteousness of our own. Faith alone is the restorative. Faith is the source—charity, that is the whole Christian life, is the stream from it."

In truth, there is no dividing the doctrines of the Church from each other. Fitly framed together in Christ's body, they grow into a holy temple to the Lord. Yet the prominence which the doctrine of faith holds in the scheme of salvation renders it a desirable and interesting subject of inquiry; and to which we consequently ask the attention of our readers.

"Faith is the evidence of things unseen." With this clear and authoritative definition extant in Holy Writ, it is not a little singular that learned and good men should differ as widely as they do in regard to the nature of faith. The difficulty arises, we apprehend, from an unrestricted use of the word, or employment of it in various senses, without sufficient regard to Scripture. When persons are not clear in their minds in regard to the exact meaning of a term, it is not wonderful that they should go astray in its use. It is difficult to analyze well. Hence, nothing is more common than for persons to take refuge in words to escape an *elenchus ignorantiæ*, or fly to synonymes to avoid a definition. In like manner, one who is better adapted to feel than to reason, when he finds his proposition oppugned, immediately repeats it, or presents it in another form, and thinks he has thus answered every objection, while he has really added nothing to what he has before said. All such processes and practices are intolerable. Words represent ideas, and must be restricted to the expression of the respective ideas which attach to them. They are the subjects of laws, and must be kept in subordination to those laws. It is a mistake to suppose that different words in the same language have exactly the same meaning. For the precise meaning of a word we must always look to the language whence it is derived, and the history and genius of the people who speak or spoke that language. Thus, a peculiar thought will be found to underlie every word. The same word, or the representative of the same idea, will necessarily be the same in every language; but it must represent the same idea. The idea of faith among one people may be very different from the idea of faith among another. The Roman's idea of faith differed not less from our idea of faith than his idea of virtue differed from our idea of virtue. The words *fides* and faith, *virtus* and virtue are in fact different words when viewed from a heathen or Christian standpoint. They are not even synonymes. It is an error, too, we may add, to suppose that synonymes are the same. Between synonymes there are always shades of difference that are both important and suggestive, and constitute no small part of the wealth of language. In fine, words must be regarded as facts, or the exponents of them, and must be dealt with accordingly. Only so can truth be attained or conserved. Let us pursue this course with our subject.

Faith, in failing to obtain generally a precise definition, has experienced the fate of other though less important words. There is no reason, however, why faith cannot be defined and reduced to proper bounds; why its orbit cannot be ascertained; why its light cannot be calculated. Educated men may differ in regard to its true acceptation, and differ honestly,—more honestly, perchance, than wisely,—but it has, like every other word, its exact place in language, its exact line of motion; it may be held, therefore, to an exact account, to move in the same direction and utter one voice. This we propose to do, relying upon Revelation to guide us in our purpose.

It has been asserted by some that faith is belief

upon probable evidence; by others, that it is absolute belief; by others, that it is unqualified assent; and by others, again, that it is perfect trust. Now, every one must feel that faith is more than all these put together. Something within man tells him that faith is not a mere feeling, that it is not a simple intellectual operation, that it is not dependent on the will, but higher, broader, and deeper; that it is intimately connected with man's spiritual life, his higher nature. What then is it?

"To credit ordinary and visible objects," says Sir Thomas Browne, "is not faith, but persuasion." The definitions of faith usually advanced assume that it is the same or the equivalent of belief more or less modified. Undoubtedly this is the popular sense in which the word is used; one in which it is, at least, a synonyme of belief. But we are not treating of faith in the common or worldly acceptation. We refer to spiritual faith, which is far different. The latter, we aver, is not belief. It is instrumental, and both in its subjective and objective relation entirely personal, while belief often relates to a subject-matter. St. Paul, during the storm (Acts xxvii. 23), said: "There stood by me this night the angel of God, whose I am, and whom I serve, saying, Fear not, Paul; thou must be brought before Cæsar: and lo, God hath given thee all them that sail with thee. Wherefore, sirs, be of good cheer: for I believe God, that it shall be even as it was told me." Why did the Apostle believe God? Because he had faith. His faith was not his belief, but the cause of it. Thus, we see, faith produces belief, which will be in proportion to the measure of the former. Faith and belief, then, are not the same; nor are they even synonymes; but they are correlatives.

"Faith," says the author of the Epistle to the Hebrews, "is the substance of things hoped for, the evidence of things unseen." It is the "substance," because its inspiring force awakens an assurance so perfect, that it is to the possessor, the element of time being omitted, a realization of hope. It is the "evidence," because it is that which enables man to believe in and lay hold upon the intangible and invisible. Faith is a cause, not an effect. It is a power, and appertains to man's spiritual nature. It is above reason, which belongs to the animal soul, and is, as Sir Thomas Browne remarks, "a rebel to faith, as passion is to reason." Finally, faith is the spirit of man excited by the Spirit of God working in things pertaining to God.

The premise of faith, the sole and only premise, is God. It is evident that man must know that God is, else he cannot have faith in him. For faith requires an object, and the highest faith demands the highest object. Abstract faith in God, or faith in a God, will not do. Some infidels, we had almost said some heathen, profess to have that, and may not be very wide of the mark. Perfect faith, Christian faith, which is the only faith of any value, is faith in Jesus Christ, both God and man. Belief in Christ and all that flows from him, belief in His Church and all that she requires, are plain correlates of faith in the Lord Jesus. "Have faith in God." Christ is God. Have faith in Christ. Hence Christianity, the Church, the Faith, are, if not precisely the same, at least synonymous.

The command, "Have faith in God," to fallen man, who is prone to evil, and whose will is at variance with that of his Maker, may seem a hard saying—one not easily complied with. But God does not require impossibilities. He has given the necessary premise; He has revealed himself directly to man; He has declared himself by His works; He has spoken in many portions and in divers manners to the fathers *in* the prophets, and to us *in* His Son. Man, therefore, being manifestly cognizant both of God and His Christ, is left without excuse. Moreover, in view of man's weakness, God has promised His holy grace to enable man to have faith. The work is man's, the power is of God. "By grace are ye saved through faith." It is the Holy Ghost that speaks to man's spirit, and strives with him for his life. Nevertheless, God does not compel man; He knocks at the door; He seeks to enter; but He does not take forcible possession. He leaves to man the elevating privilege of choice, and with it the responsibility that ensues. It follows that faith is a matter of duty, and man is faithless at his peril. Of what solemn import, then, is the question of our Lord: "When the Son of Man cometh, shall He find faith on the earth?"

Many theologians subdivide faith into four kinds,

namely, "historical, temporary, the faith of miracles, and justifying or saving faith." This classification arises, we apprehend, from confounding the operation and effect of faith with the power which is the faith. Faith can be but one, though divers operations and effects may result from it. Faith which is not inspiring, life-giving, and promotive of a right life, is only a counterfeit presentment; it is not of Christ.

In connection with our subject, we must refer to the doctrine of Justification by Faith. This is the personal application by each Christian of the whole of Christ—the God-man and his work—to himself by faith in Christ; whereby each Christian, having imputed to him the righteousness of Christ, is accounted just; what he could not otherwise be, on account of his condemned nature. Man, having no merit of his own, is freely justified by faith for Christ's sake. This comfortable doctrine is peculiar to the Christian religion, and can only consist with a free appreciation of the perfect Deity and humanity of Christ. It is the doctrine which is so dogmatically and argumentatively enforced by St. Paul. St. James has been erroneously thought by some to controvert this doctrine by laying so much stress upon justification by works. There is no disagreement, however, between the two Apostles. St. Paul had to contend incessantly with Judaism. His authoritative declarations contained in the Epistle to the Galatians, his great argument in the Epistle to the Romans, were directed to convince Jews and Judaizing Christians that man was justified not by works of the Mosaic law, nor by the law itself, but by faith in Jesus Christ. St. James presumes faith as the Christian lever, but he demands Christian works as evidences of the actual existence of faith, to avoid a possible self-delusion, or repress hypocrisy. Hence he argues that man is not justified by mere faith. The Church does not separate the two doctrines. She regards justification by works as the necessary correlative of justification by faith. They cannot exist apart. Man is justified by faith alone, in opposition to the works of the law; but as he must be "careful to maintain good works," so he is correlatively justified by works done in Christ, the merit and honor of which redound to Christ alone. Christ is all in all.

The author of the Epistle to the Hebrews, in his celebrated chapter XI., writes differently of faith, that is, in a different strain, from the Apostles we have referred to. He does not, as Alford explains, "treat of faith doctrinally, but after defining it, goes on to exhibit the triumphs of faith." There is, therefore, no want of accord, as some fancy. It would be strange indeed were there a jangling in the teaching of the one Spirit. We shall seek in vain for any such discord. The voice of the Spirit is truth itself, and the ideal of Christian life will be found ever the same throughout the pages of Revelation.

A reference to the doctrine of faith will shed light upon some of those difficulties which perplex the true believer even in regard to the conduct of God. For instance: Why does adversity so often attend, sometimes through life, the sincere Christian? Why does not prosperity always accompany those who strive to serve God? Why does not punishment tread upon the heels of the open sinner? Why do peace and prosperity so frequently accompany the unbeliever even to the end of his days? These questions include the problem of life. What explanation can we make, what answer can we give? Faith only offers an elucidation. Were God's ways open to our scrutiny, were we judges of His thoughts and actions, it is manifest that our thoughts would be measurably as His thoughts, our ways measurably as His ways. This, we know, is not the case. The dependent being cannot judge the independent Maker and Governor of the world. He must bow. "Shall not the Judge of all the earth do right?" Again: if all God's ways were unveiled, if immediate reward followed the humble believer, and immediate punishment the scorner, if the religion and ethics of God were purely mechanical, what room would there be for the exercise of faith? Religion would be man's way and not God's way. But religion is God's way, and that way is faith in Christ. "Without faith," says the Apostle, "it is impossible to please Him." Thus, faith is the key of the mystery. We cannot understand all God's ways, but by faith we can justify Him to man. Whatever mysteries cannot be unravelled, exist perfectly in accordance with reason, for the development of faith, the exercise of which inevitably conduces to the humbling of man and the setting forth of God's glory in Jesus Christ.

The vital importance, the inexorable necessity of faith as a cardinal principle in the holy religion of our Saviour Jesus Christ, is apparent from the distinct declaration of St. Paul: "Whatsoever is not of faith is sin." The reason is obvious. Purification, holiness, is the end to be attained. It is Christ's blood which cleanseth from all sin. But the "inherent righteousness of Christ cannot be wrought in us by gradual sanctification, unless the imputed righteousness of Christ be first put upon us in justification." Now, the latter, as we have said, is predicated absolutely upon faith. Both, therefore, stand by faith or fall together. Besides, man's nature being concluded under sin, his natural works are evil. The latter, however, through faith in Christ, may be sanctified by the merits of the Redeemer, and rendered acceptable to God. In fact, they thus become the works of Christ, being done in him, and good accordingly. Hence we see that in every way Christ is honored through the principle of faith.

In addition, and what must be ever borne in mind, the Holy Spirit will not abide in a faithless breast. "Grieve not the Holy Spirit;" for, when he takes His everlasting flight, we well know what spirit will enter in and dwell there. "Be not faithless, but believing."

We have now shown what we understand to be the nature, operation, influence, and effect of faith. It is one of the spiritual powers of man's higher nature quickened, as every spiritual power must be, by the Spirit of God, rendering efficient by its operation the work and teaching of Christ. It is under grace the power of God unto salvation to fallen man. By faith he believes in his heart and makes confession with his mouth; by faith he lays hold of the promises; by faith he becomes an heir of salvation; by faith he lives unto God the Father, through the medium of the life which Christ the Son lives by the Holy Spirit in the regenerate. Ought we not to fervently say with the disciples, "Lord, increase our faith?"

TRUTH.

WHAT is Truth? Whether we regard Truth as one of the attributes of the Deity, or a necessary correlative of His wisdom, it will still result that Truth appertains primarily to God; that it is His essential Nature; and that, consequently, He is the source and fountain of Truth as He is of Love and of Power. Philosophically speaking, God is both subjectively and objectively the Truth. God is not only true but He is THE TRUTH.

The highest expression of God's Truth is manifested in the person of His Son. Christ Himself is that Truth of which our Saviour spake and of which He came to bear witness. The Truth of the Son, however, is not different nor separate from the Truth of the Father and the Truth of the Holy Spirit; but as they agree in one so are they true; and as they are one so the truth is one. Christ's Truth, therefore, is God's Truth. This is the Truth, St. John says, we should "walk in;" and this is the Truth which we are assured will "make us free."

Truth, in its ordinary acceptation, apart from its source, what is commonly termed objective truth, may be classified under two heads, viz.: 1. Divine Truth; 2. Human Truth. Thus distributed, the subject can be more readily examined.

Divine Truth comprehends all the truth which the Church holds and teaches. It is but another name for Religion in its broadest sense. To elaborate the latter would be to unfold the principles and practice of Christianity. This we shall not attempt. It would take us beyond our limits and aside from our purpose, which is chiefly connected with the second division of the subject in hand.

Human Truth is the truth of the individual. It exhibits itself in its ultimate and highest form in what we may call truth of character. This feature in the moral organization of man differences not only individuals in an eminent degree, but nations. *Romana fides* was as distinct and well-defined as *Punica fides.* The one was as sure as the other was unstable. The ancients misapprehended neither. The Saxon is as naturally true as the Gascon is false. We need run the parallel no further. Truth, like courage, is a radical peculiarity. It may be developed and strengthened, but it cannot be created. No genius will produce courage. The innate coward can never be made brave, and the innately crooked mind can never be made straight. These and similar defects in the natural constitution of man, may be modified, but they cannot be eradicated, for they exist in the groundwork of character, which even "grace," as Dean Trench observes, does not "dissolve." Truth of character we assume to be that natural substratum of truth in the moral organization which begets, as far as the nature will permit, a native integrity, and when developed by sound religious culture, inevitably leads to the generation of a just conscientiousness. It is the sum, the essence of human truth. It is the measure of man's natural uprightness, his natural adaptation to good, and differences him among his fellows.

The man who possesses a native truth of character vivified by the Holy Spirit—the latter is indispensable, owing to human nature being fallen through sin—feels an almost instinctive repugnance to the false. He loves the truth for the truth's sake. He recoils from deceit. Nothing can induce him to practise it. Observe his life and conversation. He never says more than he knows, nor expresses more than he feels. He never exaggerates, nor improves, nor adds, nor diminishes, nor "extenuates, nor sets down aught in malice;" but in all cases and under all circumstances, be they great or small, concern they himself or others, he adheres tenaciously to the simple truth in its fulness. Nor only in the letter does he this, but in the spirit likewise. In fact, he endeavors to think the truth, to live the truth, and thus to be a true man.

Job is a fine example of natural truth of character. Daniel is another. Socrates, in the Pagan world, may rank as a third. Among Christians, apart from inspired men, we know of no more distinguished instance than that of Washington. Truth should ever be awakened into life by the Holy Spirit and fostered by Christian nurture. St. Paul very beautifully calls this principle quickened by the Word, in its activity, "truthing it in love." (Eph. iv. 15.) We know not how the idea of Christian truth of character could be more exactly expressed. The man who always strives to truth it in love will certainly be true as far as fallen man can be. Honor, honesty, rectitude, uprightness, integrity, probity—all find their common centre in Truth. By it and in it they all consist. Each one is but the Truth in action either generally or specifically; and regarding honesty as a generic term, comprehending every phase of Truth, whether in principle, in thought, or in act, the often-disputed words of the poet are absolutely true,—

"An honest man 's the noblest work of God."

Aberrations from Truth, of whatsoever kind, will be found, upon examination, to exhibit a defect in truth of character. Where the character is true, little apprehension of falling into error need be felt; for the Truth, then, is sought, known, and appreciated well-nigh instinctively. But where the character is not true, doubts are apt to arise concerning truth as a whole or some feature of it. Apparent truth is too often mistaken or substituted for real truth; and in fact, Truth, instead of being held as an "immutable principle," is argued out of existence or quite dispensed with as a variable quantity. For instance, there are many who verily appear to think that there is no deceit in acting what is false, provided nothing is said that is untrue. There are not a few, too, who fondly imagine that falsehoods can be consecrated by custom and thus rendered equivalent to truths. Every branch of society, every part in life, however high or however low, seems to be pervaded by these baneful errors. Their unhappy influence is manifested everywhere. It is seen in the *nolo episcopari* which has passed into a proverb, in the professional conscience, in political usage, in literary practice, in business custom, in the modes of the world, and in the manners of society. The universality of measurably legalized insincerity is melancholy. To be incapable of saying what one really thinks is, perhaps, rare, but to be capable of saying what one does not think, is comparatively common. Now all this proceeds from that prevalent deficiency in truth of character to which we have before referred. The most refined insincerity, the grossest falseness may be with equal certainty traced to this fault. But where truth of character exists, there is true thinking, true speaking, and true acting; there is no lie. The importance, therefore, of grounding truth in the character,—some characters, be it remembered, have a larger capacity for truth than others,—that the whole man may be true and exemplify the Truth, is self-evident. We will only add the enforcement of Polonius, whose "precept" on this subject every man would do well to "character in his memory."

> "To thine ownself be true;
> And it must follow, as the night the day,
> Thou canst not then be false to any man."

Whence comes it that thorough truth of character is rare? Notwithstanding the proneness to deceit which is incident to man's fallen nature, there is a great deal of truth in the world,—more truth, in the aggregate, according to the status of human nature, we apprehend, than falsehood; but there is not a great deal of truth of character. Why is this? One reason is, that the Father of lies is constantly on the alert to promote deceit and obstruct the course of Truth in every shape. The potency of his agency will not be doubted by any who regards Satan as a reality. He began his work upon earth with a lie and by that lie he perverted man's hitherto upright nature and caused an undue development of selfishness which teaches the justifying means by ends, of temper which overthrows the reason, of pride and vanity which ensnare the heart, of self-will which blinds the eyes to the truth and leads men captive,—in fine, to all those features of character which are contrary to the Truth and "war against the soul." Another reason is, the refusal to recognize the unity of Truth,—the habit of dividing Truth, not as we have done formally for the sake of analysis, but practically, and thus in a degree ignoring it. For instance, it is common for persons to take a part of the Truth, *e. g.*, the habit of speaking the truth, or its negative correlate, the custom of not saying what is false, and consider that as the sum of Truth. Thus, they who maintain a proper respect for their word are deemed truthful. It must be confessed, the habit of speaking the truth is most excellent. We would not underrate its importance. Indeed, we incline "to the opinion of those who have held that Truth is an eternal and immutable principle; and probably whatever extraordinary instances may sometimes occur, where some evil may be prevented by violating this noble principle, it would be found that human happiness would, upon the whole, be more perfect were Truth universally preserved." But the habit of speaking the truth, though indispensable, is not the whole of Truth, nor does it constitute, necessarily, a person truthful in the full sense of the term. Great punctiliousness in that respect may, and often does, coexist with decided falseness both in thought and action. Motive must not be left out of the account. One person may speak the truth from right principle; another, because it is his principle, or from an abstract love of truth,—which is quite deceptive, as a man thus sometimes merely "loves," as Bishop Warburton well remarks, "his own opinions," or what he assumes to be his; a third, for the sake of convenience,—it is a most convenient habit, as one who always speaks the exact truth need not remember what he says, nor fear his words rising up in judgment against him; a fourth, from motives of mere expediency. Certainly it is better to speak the truth for the two reasons last mentioned, or, perhaps, any, than to lie. A negative goodness is preferable to a positive sin; for no evil may spring from the former, whereas wrong must accompany the latter. But the truth of a man who is influenced by low motives will not survive the latter. It will not endure trial nor persecution. But the truth of a man who speaks the truth for the Truth's sake, who is inwardly true, humanly speaking, will endure forever. The making the habit of speaking the truth a matter of convenience or expediency is very far from being truthful. It is near akin to the ethics of interest and not very far removed from that morality which consecrates everything by the object in view. Christian ethics has higher motives and nobler aims. But even the habit of speaking the truth in all honesty, so far from comprehending the Truth in its entirety, is but one offspring of that inward Truth which we conceive to be the abstract of human Truth, and which itself needs sanctification by Divine Truth as the second table of the law (the second commandment of Christ), needs spiritualizing by the first.

There are some, we are sorry to say, who practically, though, perhaps, not always advisedly, ignore the Truth. We refer to those who boast a charity so large that it elevates them above, and renders them independent, if not oblivious, of the Truth. Such persons will discard the distinctive tenets of the Church, disregard the dictates of right judgment, dispute the credibility of Revelation, or deny the truth of Christianity, under cover of their professed liberality of mind, their enlarged charity. But, as Dr. Wordsworth writes, "Truth is the greatest charity. It is no charity to connive at error, and to suppress Truth; but it is charity (love) to endeavor to remove error and to maintain and communicate Truth." The charity of the persons alluded to is like the catholicity of sectarians; the one is a charity without life, the other a catholicity of error; both are "counterfeit presentments," and, therefore, equally void of Truth. Pity it is that so many are led astray, as we fear there are, by such "saintly shows." The recollection that Truth and Charity are more than twins—they cannot exist apart—would prevent many evil deeds being done in the name of the latter.

In connection with our subject we must not omit to notice one singular fact. It is that Truth can be so perverted that it will savor of sin. For example: when what, for the sake of convenience, we have styled "Human Truth," is made a religion of and substituted for the religion of Christ, it becomes like a brazen serpent, an idol and sin to them who bow down to it. All who deny Jesus Christ—the God-Man—of whatever character or complexion, from the mild, moral, milk-fed sceptic, to the bold, meat-eating infidel,—all split upon this rock. Thus the man whose whole life is a lie will prate about his reverence for Truth. Truth, he proudly affirms, is his religion. Not God's Truth, nor the Truth which is of God, and which, like the "rivers that run into the sea," in its flux and reflux, "returns whence it came," but his own truth—the truth which he vainly imagines is in himself and part of his nature. Hence he becomes a god unto himself and "worships the creature more than the Creator." Truth, however, is not destroyed by being misapprehended or denied; it is of God, and must exist forever, and will make itself known. Study to be true, even true in Christ.

We have said that dividing the Truth, especially the custom of separating Divine from human Truth, is eminently productive of error. Truth is God in its highest sense; and it is of God in that position and relation where, as Cousin says, it lies "between human intelligence and the Supreme Intelligence, as a kind of mediator." Truth, therefore, cannot be many, as error is many; it must be one; and to divide it positively, causes untruth in all that multiplicity and variety of manifestation which would require a volume to describe and which we can only deplore.

How can Truth be promoted? We answer: The Truth and the truths which the "Church of the living God, the pillar and ground of the Truth," receives from God and dispenses to man for his edification in Christ must, first of all, be appropriated and assimilated by man. Then will Christ be formed in man by the power of the Holy Spirit—the Spirit of Truth; then will human truth be energized by the Truth itself; then will truth of character be generated and the whole man become true as far as he can be in this world; for the Truth itself will be in action in and through man, and will finally make him free from everything that worketh falsehood. Man should remember always that God is omniscient and omnipresent. He inspects his thoughts and observes his acts. Man may delude himself or impose upon his fellow, but he cannot deceive God. He knows what is in man—when he errs, and when he thinks and speaks and acts the truth. Man should walk as in the sight of God, making a conscience of his ways. Being human, he must walk waywardly, but under Christ he will walk uprightly if he sanctify the Lord God in his heart, and "truth" it with his neighbor in love.

LOVE AND CHARITY.

Words are the representatives of ideas; but they are often interchangeably used, and in various senses; thus the same word is frequently made to convey a variety of ideas, accordingly as it may be employed. To illustrate this we will adduce a few examples, and then proceed to the more particular consideration of the theme embodied in the words we have placed at the head of this paper.

The word life, in the Scriptures, is sometimes used to express the life by which, or in which, we live,—the life of Christ in the regenerate, which is the true life of the redeemed man. Life often is a term for the character and course of man's daily walk, his existence upon earth; thus it is said to be happy or unhappy, good or evil, long or short. Life is frequently used as the antithesis of spiritual death, and as the opposite of physical death. When St. Paul says of "godliness," that it has the "promise of the life that now is and that which is to come," he uses the word, as Trench has shown from the original, in the first sense. Attention to this would enlighten the eyes of many in regard to that beautiful passage of the philosophic Apostle. When Jacob says, with entire truth, "few and evil have the days of my life been," he uses the word in the second sense. When God said, "in the day thou eatest thereof thou shalt surely die," He referred to spiritual death—the death of man's spiritual life. This life was restored by the agency of the Incarnation; but it is also necessary for man to be regenerated, born again of water and the Spirit, in order to enter the kingdom of heaven. The other senses ascribed to this word are too familiar to need elucidation.

Soul is another word in point. Sometimes it describes the entire man, as "eight souls were saved" in the ark; sometimes it refers to the animal soul which man has in common with the brutes, and to which St. Paul refers when he speaks of "body, soul, and spirit;" and often it represents the spirit, man's immortal part, —"I saw under the altar," says St. John, "the souls of them that were slain," etc.

Religion, virtue, truth, piety are words which are also employed in a variety of senses, sometimes interchangeably. No one, however, need be at a loss in regard to the correct meaning of each. The New Testament, with the Prayer Book as a commentary, will guide every one, who does not prefer to wander, in the straight path. They are enough for definition and practice.

We might adduce further examples of the different

modes in which words are employed, making them convey one idea at one time and another at another; but we have said enough to establish the point in question, and we will now come to the contemplation of those words which we wish more particularly to discuss, which we think will be found both interesting and suggestive. We refer to Love and Charity, the theme of St. Paul's thirteenth chapter of First Corinthians, by many thought to be the most beautiful portion of the writings of the Apostle that have come down to us.

The English language has two main sources termed generically the Saxon and the Latin. Hence it is two-sided in its general aspect, and words for the same thoughts and things are found in it which proceeded respectively from the above sources. After English had established itself as the vernacular of the nation, its twofold character was marked and maintained by the Anglo-Normans adhering to the Latin side of the language, while the lower classes naturally made use of the Saxon. Two modes of speaking, therefore, grew directly out of the double extraction of the people. Many of our readers will remember Wamba's dissertation upon the subject in the first chapter of Ivanhoe. "The two idioms," says De Vere, "for a time lived side by side, though in very different conditions; the one the language of the master, at court and in the castles of the soldiers who had become noble lords and powerful barons: the other, the language of the conquered, spoken only in the lowly hut of the subjugated people." Hence, from the structure of society Norman English was considered polite, Saxon English vulgar. The one was heard in *palace* and *castle*, the other in the *home* and by the *hearth*. Time, however, changed all this. The Norman race conquered the realm, but could not extrude the language of the people. At the present day the best writers and speakers of English, on both sides of the Atlantic, cultivate the Saxon element, and rightly too, for though the Latin element adds fulness and elegance, upon the Saxon depend the strength and terseness of the language. The King James translation of the Bible, and the Prayer Book, we need hardly say, are admirable illustrations of these points. They exhibit the elegance of the Roman and the strength of the Teutonic.

In the compound character of the English language, to a desire to meet the wants of the *palace* and the *cottage*, to a wish to reach the *affections* and the *hearts* of a people thus descended from too sources, whose vernacular was the result of the fusion of two idioms, may be attributed the duplicate expressions so frequent in the Liturgy of the Church. These iterations, we must admit, are sometimes merely redundancies; they do not always spring from the union of a Saxonism and a Latinism, as "assemble and meet together," "pardon and forgive," but are all one or the other, as "goodness and kindness," "acknowledge and confess." Nevertheless the use of duplicate phrases, and doubtless a majority of the phrases themselves, came from the cause we have described. They form a marked feature in the literary style of the Prayer Book, and though unnecessary now, as the people have become one in language, they add such a grace to the Liturgy, and give it a rhythm so peculiar to itself, that no one with a particle of taste would consent to spare them from its pages.

The expression "love and charity" is a good example of what we have endeavored to unfold. The first is a Saxon, the second a Greek word. Both, however, are identical in meaning. Unfortunately, the latter has been diverted from its true and original sense, and has come to be used in that of alms-giving. As St. James gives the name of "religion" to some of the genuine fruits of that power and principle, so persons constantly style eleemosynary duty, charity; whereas charity denotes properly that benevolence of feeling which prompts man to relieve the wants of his neighbor. It is so far a cause, not an effect. Still the true meaning of the word is not lost; it survives the common metonyme, and its double acceptation need not produce any confusion in the mind. Besides, as we have shown, charity is not the only word that is employed in more ways than one.

In the Church service the phrase "love and charity" is merely the combination of a Saxon and a Greek word which was introduced to enforce upon all the one idea and duty—love. The words are not synonymes, which always contain a shade of difference in their meaning, but simply two distinct words, derived from two distinct languages, and convey exactly the same idea. They must be regarded, therefore as one—love. Hence "to be in love and charity with one's neighbors," is simply to love them. Love is the element of Christianity,—that in which it "lives and moves and has its being." Thus it is not unreasonable that the followers of Christ should be required to love one another, and that love should be made a condition of holy communion, the highest act of the Faith.

But what is the love taught by our Saviour and His Apostles; the love which is esteemed by St. Paul in 1 Corinthians, ch. 13, as the crowning grace? It is not the passion generally understood by that word; it is not merely the feeling called affection; it is not the sentiment implied in the word esteem. No; it is Christian love—*agape*. Rather an emotion than a passion, it has no relation to age, sex, or condition. We may define it negatively by saying that it is the antithesis of malice. Yet it is positive in character, active as well as sentient; for its fountain is God, the source of all love, who "first loved us and gave His only begotten Son"— God with Him—"to die for our sins." Hence our first love is due to God, our second to our neighbor. Under the influence of this principle the sincere Christian rightly strives to perform his duty to God—for thus only can he love Him—and his duty to his fellow man, as a proof of his love to God. Love, we may add, is also the *state* which necessarily ensues from the exercise of duty rightly performed. In one sense, therefore, it is a cause, and in another an effect.

It must not be supposed that Christian love is an absolute moral solvent. On the contrary it involves no negation of individuality. It leaves each one free to choose his own associates, to form his own habits, to pursue his own plans and pleasures, provided, in so doing, he trespass not upon the rights and feelings of others. Neither has Christian love the least sympathy with sin. It entertains no accord with that spurious Charity, unhappily too prevalent, which under pretence of enlarged views, liberal ideas, generous feelings or kind relations, exhibits disregard of principles and manifests indifference to error. Christian love burns for the sinner, but keeps no terms with his sin. Christian charity is truthful, even as its source is true.

Amid the manifold circumstances of this life, surrounded by various characters, man cannot always expect to be at peace. Sin is in the world, and sin is the enemy of peace. Besides, wrong-doing awakens indignation as properly as right-doing does admiration. Both feelings are sentiments that belong to every honest, rightly constituted mind. Our Saviour, our ultimate example, exhibited both as circumstances demanded. All that can be asked of the person who endeavors to fulfil the second commandment of Christ, which is always a consequence of the first, is that, "as far as possible, he should live peaceably with all men." He should neither give, nor too hastily take offence; he should, without presupposing an abrogation of any of the commandments of God, endeavor to do as he would that another should do unto him. If he chance to sin against a neighbor, he can be brave enough and humble enough to confess his sin unto God, and honest enough to do what may lie in his power to reconcile himself to his neighbor. Should he sustain an injury which the law will not remedy—for every man is entitled to the protection of the law and may resort to it in due season, upon due provocation—he has only to bear with Christian resignation the wrong which he has received, knowing that his Divine Master submitted to far greater outrages for him than he can be called upon to endure, and hold himself ever ready to meet the transgressor in the spirit of peace, whenever the latter shall open the door in the spirit of harmony and truth. Love asks no fusion of right and wrong, of truth and falsehood. It is noble and just in all its ways.

Christian love or charity is a pure moral feeling, and may be summed up, we apprehend, in the apostolic injunction: "Be ye kindly affectioned one towards another." Presupposing faith, this is the principle which should govern men. Faith should work by love. Love tempers judgment with mercy, strengthens the feeble knees, supports the hands that are ready to fall; it joys with another's joy and grieves with another's grief; it comprehends the inestimable charm of sympathy—a very bond of union; and, were it possible, would liken earth to heaven. Be careful, therefore, to banish all malice and jealousy from the heart, to preserve kind and just feelings and maintain honest conduct towards all men, that being, as all should be, members of Christ's body, ye may be in love and charity with your neighbors, meet partakers of His holy feast, and certified heirs of the joy to be revealed —the joy of the Lord which no man can take from you. Blessed be God for His unspeakable gift to His faithful people in Jesus Christ.

CONSCIENCE.

Man is responsible for his thoughts as well as for his acts; for an act is but the fruition of a thought. To think rightly, therefore, is of the first importance in the government of life. Nothing tends more certainly to prevent correct thinking than a false or even lax use of words. Persons frequently employ them in such inaccurate or various senses that they neither understand themselves nor comprehend others. De Quincey, who is distinguished by elegance of style and exactness of diction, has shown in several instances the evil effect generated by a careless use of words. Thus, we constantly hear it said, that such a theory is right, but that it will not hold good in practice. Now a theory is a rule derived from the "looking over" of certain facts. It is an induction from practice. Consequently, if facts enough be given and the induction be logical, what is true in theory must be true in practice. The error arises from confounding *theory* with *hypothesis*—a very common error which confuses many. How frequently, too, do we hear persons who never formed an opinion in their lives on any important matter—that is, arrived at a sound conclusion by right reasoning from just premises—talk about their opinions on such and such subjects; whereas they mean their crude notions or prejudices—prejudgments. Such persons may, and often very wisely do, adopt the opinions of others. We are charitable enough to believe that they sometimes mistake them for their own. But, in truth, they entertain no opinions that can be called their own in a proper sense. Only thinking people form opinions, while all have prejudices. We may add, that as *recta ratio est vera lex*, "right reasoning is true law," so only right-minded persons who employ right modes of thought will form right opinions.

Conscience is another word, important as it is, which has not succeeded in securing for itself such accurate signification and use that the wayfaring man cannot err in regard to it. One person thinks conscience an internal monitor, the operation of which however he cannot satisfactorily explain; another regards conscience as an operation of the mind akin to judgment; a third considers conscience itself of no importance, as its character depends upon education, and what may be right in one may be wrong in another; while a fourth determines conscience to be the Holy Spirit in man, and therefore incapable of error. Out of this confusion, this mixture of the true and the false, flows an indistinct conception of the term which may be productive of evil. Fortunately knowledge and practice do not always go together. Doubtless there are some who, philologically speaking, do not know what conscience is, and yet are more conscientious than many learned pundits. Still ignorance is not to be argued for, and it will not injure the force of a word to have it defined, but rather increase its value.

Denfiition, says Dean Trench somewhere, is a serious affair. It is so; for upon sharp definitions correct thinking depends. Misty words are the inevitable vehicle of misty thoughts. "It is more dangerous to define than to describe," says the elder D'Israeli; "a dry definition excludes so much, an ardent description at once appeals to our sympathies." This is true; but description too often leaves the word described in so much of a fog that the reader is little wiser than before. Witness the numerous descriptions of genius. Who does not long for a definition when he reads one of these sympathetic descriptions. In truth, definition and description should go together: the former should always precede the latter.

Conscience deserves more than a "dry definition;" and it should not be left in the fog of a "sympathetic description." We believe that it can be defined and illustrated. That we propose to do. By the aid of Dr. Adams's work on "Christian Science" we will endeavor to explain the nature of conscience and its mode of action—in a word, elaborate it.

We premise that there is a conscience. The consentient voice of Scripture testifies to the fact; experience proves it. It is a faculty of the spiritual reason, an organ of man's highest nature. This faculty, like any other, may remain dormant, or may receive a right or wrong development, according to circumstances. Man, however, living under the light of the Gospel, with the Word of God to guide him, is responsible for having a good conscience. He cannot escape from the obligation. Certainly, if in the days of the Apostles, the converted heathen were required to maintain a "conscience void of offence toward God and toward man," as much may reasonably be demanded of the Christians of the present day. We insist, therefore, that man has been endowed by his Maker with a conscience, and that he can, and necessarily is obligated to, preserve it enlightened and active. Were this not the case conscience might as well not exist.

But how does conscience operate? What is its mode of action? Let us examine.

First, it is not the Holy Spirit in man, but the organ whereby the Holy Spirit, external to man, exerts his holy influence to guide and restrain man. Hence, if the still small voice speak in accordance with the commandments of our Saviour Christ—for even if a miracle were to speak otherwise it would be but a "lying wonder,"—it must be heeded; since we are expressly told by the Apostle, who asserts that there is a conscience, that we must "not grieve the Holy Spirit."

Second, the mode in which conscience acts is three-fold, viz.:

1. "It prohibits."
2. "It records."
3. "It prophesies." *

The special and most marked peculiarity of conscience is its first or prohibitory feature. Thus, when we are doing, or going to do right, we are not conscious of possessing a conscience: but let us propose to do wrong; immediately conscience rises up and says—*No.* Reflection may furnish reasons for this opposition on the part of conscience and sustain its negative; but prior to their consideration conscience said, *Do it not,* and that, too, without affording the slightest reason. The latter must be sought; conscience need not. It speaks as the occasion demands. *Nil conscire sibi, nulla pallescere culpa*—to be conscious of no fault—is the only way to preserve a *quiet* conscience.

The story of Balaam (Num. xxii.) quite pointedly illustrates the negative feature, and if it were not a true history, might be regarded as a parable of conscience. Balak, king of Moab, alarmed at the invasion of the children of Israel, sent messengers to Balaam, a notable prophet, praying that he would come and curse the approaching host. Before acceding to the request of the king, Balaam awaited to receive counsel of the Lord. God appeared to him that night and forbad

* Adams's "Christian Science."

him either to go with the messengers or curse the people. Balaam obeyed in both particulars. On receiving an answer in the negative, Balak sent more honorable messengers urging the prophet to come and promising him great rewards. Balaam again awaited to learn the counsel of the Lord before yielding to the king's request. God appeared to Balaam that night and directed him to go, but only to say what He should give him to say. Balaam obeyed in one particular. He went; but he went to do the bidding of Balak and not of God. Hence God's wrath was kindled, and the Angel of Jehovah withstood the prophet in his perverse way and compelled him to go and bless the children of Israel as He had commanded him. Just so conscience withstands every one who attempts to do wrong; only, unlike the angel in the path, conscience can be disregarded or ridden over. "A good conscience," says an old French writer, "is the best guardian angel."

Shakspeare, who never was at a loss where human nature is concerned, finely exhibits the operation of conscience in the "Merchant of Venice." Launcelot is cogitating whether he shall run away from his master. "Certainly my conscience will serve me to run from this Jew, my master. The fiend is at mine elbow, and tempts me, saying to me, *Gobbo, Launcelot Gobbo, good Launcelot, or good Gobbo, or good Launcelot Gobbo, use your legs, take the start, run away.* My conscience says—*No; take heed, honest Launcelot; take heed, honest Gobbo; or*, as aforesaid, *honest Launcelot Gobbo:*

do not run; scorn running with thy heels. Well, the most courageous fiend bids me pack; *via!* says the fiend; *away!* says the fiend, *for the heavens; rouse up a brave mind*, says the fiend, *and run.* Well, my conscience hanging about the neck of my heart, says very wisely to me,—*My honest friend Launcelot, being an honest man's son*—my conscience says, *Launcelot, budge not; budge*, says the fiend; *budge not*, says my conscience: Conscience, say I, you counsel well; fiend, say I, you counsel well; to be ruled by my conscience, I should stay with the Jew my master, who (God bless the mark!) is a kind of devil; and to run away from the Jew, I should be ruled by the fiend, who, saving your reverence, is the devil himself. Certainly, the Jew is the very devil incarnation; and, in my conscience, my conscience is but a hard kind of conscience, to offer to counsel me to stay with the Jew. The fiend gives the more friendly counsel. I will run, fiend; my heels are at your commandment, I will run."

Thus we see that conscience utters her voice in opposition; but her voice may be unheeded; arguments may be and often are found, for disregarding her warnings. The conduct of Launcelot excellently illustrates this.

We have said that conscience is threefold. The negative character which marks its first division likewise pervades its two other features. Thus, whether it record the nature of a past act, or prophesy the consequences that will ensue from that act, or indeed, any act, it always does so when the act is wrong, never when it is right. In the latter case conscience is quiescent; precisely as it is when it is proposed to do right. An approving conscience is not apparent on an analysis, and may be resolved into a conventional phrase. In fact, approval of either thought or act is only an exercise of an enlightened judgment in the premises. Conscience is quite another matter. So far from being, as Dr. Sharp declares, "nothing else but a man's judgment or persuasion concerning moral good or evil, or concerning what he ought to do, and what he ought not to do, and what he may lawfully do," it is a faculty which remains at rest, and of which we are entirely unconscious until it arises, on a sudden, full armed, to combat and condemn.

Let us examine further into the movements and bearing of conscience. "God has given us," says Bishop Taylor, "conscience to be in His stead to us, to give us laws, and to exact obedience of those laws, to punish them that prevaricate, and to reward the obedient. And therefore conscience is called the household guardian, the domestic god, the spirit or angel of the place; and when we call God to witness, we only mean that our conscience is right, and that God and God's vicar, our conscience, knows it." This view of conscience does not harmonize with what we have said. It makes conscience an enlightened, internal judge, that acts affirmatively or negatively, and rewards or condemns according to circumstances. Whereas we have shown that conscience is strictly privative in its action, whether it refer to the past, the present, or the future. As to calling God to witness—swearing by the name of the Lord—being merely an assertion that the conscience of the person so doing is right, in our judgment it is something far different and far more solemn. Taking an oath is a full recognition that God is, and that He will visit a perjurer far beyond what conscience has the power to do. Conscience is not awake enough in some people to punish even perjury; but God never sleeps, and will not permit His Name to be taken in vain.

Besides, it is to be observed with respect to the action of conscience, that it bears only indirectly upon affairs here. Reason, or the affections, will indicate the quality of an act in its relation to this world merely, but conscience takes cognizance of it with reference to the next. For instance, take the mean maxim, *Honesty is the best policy*,—we say, "mean," for man should be honest because it is right and not because it is politic. "Fontenelle, seeing a man led to punishment, said, 'there is a man who has calculated badly,' whence it follows," continues Cousin, "that if this man, in doing what he did, could have escaped punishment, he would have calculated well, and his conduct would have been laudable. The action then becomes good or ill according to the issue. Every act is of itself indifferent, and it is lot that qualifies it. If the honest is only the useful, the genius of calculation is the highest wisdom; it is even virtue! Rather do what you ought, come what may." Take for example, we say, the sordid maxim referred to, the sum of the ethics of interest. The shrewd, unscrupulous, selfish man is apt to prosper in the business of this world. Hence it is inferred by some short-sighted people that honesty is *not* the best policy. Reason will point out to the selfish man the material advantages which rapidly accrue to an over-reaching policy; and affection for himself and his, will stimulate him onward in the path which seems to promise prosperity and power. Here the two organs of the animal soul—the natural reason and affection—are sufficient to show the way, and would undoubtedly, in every case, set the will in motion to carry into effect the fair-seeming policy. But conscience, a power of the spiritual reason or higher nature, starts up, if alive, and objects. When heeded, reflection follows and says in support of conscience, "selfishness and dishonesty may perhaps do for this world, but they will not answer for the world to come. Look ahead,—honesty is the best policy, future accountability taken into consideration." Thus, as Dr. Adams remarks, "conscience is the perception of good or evil in action with reference to a future responsibility." It may, therefore, be justly considered as the guardian angel in the breast.

In justice to Dr. Adams, whose work on "Christian Science" we have both used and quoted, we would refer our readers to his chapter on the subject we have been discussing. No one will peruse it without pleasure and few without profit. Would that Hamlet's reflection—

"Conscience does make cowards of us all,"

were true in all cases. Not that cowardice is a commendable trait; but too many "brave," as Montaigne says, "toward God and cowards toward man," or, alas! weak, think, like Launcelot, that the "fiend gives the more friendly counsel." Nor is this to be wondered at when we reflect that the archfiend Satan himself is continually on the watch, seeking to poison the thoughts and pervert the ways of each child of Adam, and well knows the weakest points of each, and how he may be most successfully assailed. Conscience, however, is a safeguard which God has furnished to protect every one against the wiles of the adversary, and the sins which do so easily beset mankind. Happy are they who listen to the voice of Conscience—that "cry of the soul"—as Cousin beautifully terms it, and give heed to its divine warnings. They will not experience the inevitable bite of the roused serpent; they will not have to look forward with dread to the fearful panorama of sin which the quickened memory will, with its daguerreotype power, one day unfold, before their grieved eyes; they will be at peace with themselves; they will be followers of Christ, and at unity with God.

Though conscience is a faculty of the moral nature, as much as memory is of the intellectual, practically a right development of the power is necessary to insure its just action. No good can be predicated of ignorance; none ought to be. We live in the light, and if we will, we can have our consciences enlightened that they may be sound guides and void of offence. "If," as Alford finely observes, "we must be taught of God, we must also learn of God." The responsibility rests with us.

This being granted, it is asked; what rule shall govern us in the formation of a good conscience?—We answer briefly: "Render unto Cæsar the things which be Cæsar's, and unto God the things which be God's." Reader, so doing, in the first, you will be a good citizen—a good neighbor; in the second, a good Christian—a true Churchman; in both an honest man. You cannot be more, you should not aim to be less. So live then that you will be enabled to say with the Apostle: "Oure glorie is this, the witnessyng of oure *conscience*, that in symplenesse and clennesse of God and not in fleischli wisdom but in the grace of God we lyuyden in this world."

PROVIDENCE.

We remarked once to a gentleman, an educated man—one who had studied theology outside of the Church—that we could not conceive how any intelligent person could look at external nature and consider its wonder, its beauty, and its variety, and profess to be an *Atheist.* "Perhaps you do not know," replied he unhesitatingly, "that I am one." We were not a little startled at the confession and at the coolness with which it was made. Nevertheless we doubted its truth. We think that such an avowal must spring either from singular ignorance or diabolical perversion of the faculties, or both. We do not believe that any sane person is really at heart an atheist. It is true sceptics are shallow thinkers, though they seem to

> " . . . Dive into the bottom of the deep,
> Where fathom line could never touch,"

to those who never think, and thus sometimes get befogged themselves and befog others. It is true, too, that many are practically atheists—that is, as Bishop Short says, "they are not influenced in what they do by any fixed principles which refer to a future responsibility. Practically, they do not believe in the undoubted truth that we shall all hereafter be judged according as we have conducted ourselves in this life. Their minds may be so far convinced that they may not be prepared to controvert the position; but if we look at their conduct with reference to a day of judgment, as a question of fact, it would be very difficult to prove that they did believe in a future state." There are many, also, with whom "the wish is father to the thought;" they hope there is no God. But, at heart, something tells them that there is a God. They can not escape from the internal revelation which the Creator makes of Himself by His Spirit to all mankind. As a rule, therefore, we believe that we are justified in claiming that all persons of sound mind believe in a personal God.

There are, however, some, even within the circle of professed believers, who, quite unintentionally, project themselves into the cold and shoreless region of atheism. Such are they who, while they confess to a belief in Divine Providence—which is only a general or theistic appellation of Deity—and admit that He exerts a general providence in the affairs of this world, deny that He ever exercises a special or particular providence in regard to them. The untenableness of the position can be easily shown. For instance: the general providence of God can be nothing more than the aggregate of His special or particular providences.* Hence to disbelieve in special providences is to disbelieve in the general providence of God. To disbelieve in the latter is to deny the attributes of God, and consequently to deny Him, which is atheism. The converse of the proposition is equally true, viz.: to believe in special providence is to believe in general providence, and so in God. The logic is incontrovertible, the conclusion must be accepted.

But, apart from the logic of the case, the idea that God made the world and then left it, is absurd; that He subordinated it to certain laws, which thus became as God to it, is equally unreasonable. Such a system would set God afar off. It would annihilate man's personal relation with his Maker. God's benevolence would be destroyed. It would find no place to act. God might be the Great, but He would not be the Good God who "keepeth covenant and sheweth mercy." God could not then be Love.

Yet it is not to be inferred from what we have said that the Almighty never does act through general laws. On the contrary, God has ordained such laws, both moral and physical in their character, and fortified by sanctions to secure to them respect and obedience on the part of man. If a city or an army neglect proper sanatory regulations, disease and death follow. If an

* Dr. Francis Vinton. Unpublished sermon.

individual set at defiance the laws of his physical being, retribution will sooner or later overtake him. If he violate the principles of sound thinking, if he indulge a prurient imagination, mental and moral deterioration will be the result. If the natural laws of trade and commerce are disregarded, public prosperity declines, financial disorders, often acting and reacting throughout the whole commercial world and sometimes involving governments, ensue. A moderate acquaintance with science and history proves what we have asserted. Now, in such and all similar cases we need not assume that the punishment inflicted, apparently by the overruling hand, is anything more (though it may be) than the sanction attached to, and the necessary consequence of, the violation of the general law. It neither detracts from the majesty of God nor from the truth of the doctrine affirmed, that the Almighty impresses general laws upon His creation and enforces those laws. What we aver is, that God is not limited by such laws, but in accordance with the truth of His nature does always and in such mode as He prefers, what is right in His eyes.

There is another argument in confirmation of the truth of the doctrine of special providence which we regard as completely irrefragable. Without this doctrine what becomes of Christ and His Church? Is not Christ the First of all God's special as well as general providences? Is not the scheme of Redemption the grandest of all special providences that can be conceived of? Is not the work of the Holy Spirit in man a continual special providence? If these are not, we confess that we are at a loss to know what are special providences. Besides, who can read the Scriptures without seeing this doctrine ingrained throughout them? If the very existence of the Jew is an attestation to the truth of Revelation, it is also a confirmation of the truth of the doctrine in question.

Further, if the doctrine be not true, if there be no special providences, what is the purport and object of prayer? It must be idle and aimless and therefore profane. But we are commanded to pray. "Ask and you shall receive." We have been also taught to pray; and many will admit that when they have prayed with faith and earnestness their prayers have been graciously responded to. No one who has had any varied and extended experience in Christian life, or in any kind of life, but will avow that God constantly exhibits His working in particular providences. No argument will stagger the Christian in his belief in regard to this doctrine. He knows that it is true; his convictions have become a part of himself.

Notwithstanding, we find not a few in every Christian community, who, perhaps without intending it, substantially ignore the doctrine of special or particular providences. For instance, when we listen to the anathemas poured out upon the weather by some persons —dissatisfaction with the heat, disgust at the cold, annoyance with the drought, disappointment at the rain, irritation with the wind, vexation at the calm—we might imagine that in their opinion some factiously-elected demagogue controlled the elements and governed the weather. We would hardly infer from their expressions that they believed that it was the Lord who "caused the grass to grow, the vapors to ascend, the wind to blow, and the waters to flow, the rain to descend upon one city and not upon another, and did whatever He pleased in heaven, in earth, and in the sea."

Again, when a distinguished man dies at a peculiar time, when the public seem to need his services in his vocation, his death is deplored, the loss is deemed fearful, the calamity irreparable, and many, in fact, really appear to think the Almighty has committed an error in removing so valuable an individual at so important a juncture. Do such persons truly recognize the hand of Providence in what they esteem a calamity of such singular magnitude? Do they reflect that had God needed the services of the deceased either in Church or State or private life, He would have preserved him to do His will? Do they remember that God made man simply to honor Himself; that it is He who kills and He who makes alive; that He who could spare Moses could provide Joshua; and in fine, that all things are His from the smallest to the greatest, and that there is nothing without Him?

How often, too, do we see persons who have lost relatives appearing for years draped in black; thereby evincing their determination to mourn, openly at least, without limit for those whom God has taken away. Now the external signs of grief prescribed by the laws of Christian society are decent in themselves and in accordance with the spirit of true religion; but mourning, when continued beyond the period usually allotted by the custom of society, is not only an exhibition of bad taste, but an ostentatious parade of external woe that is above recognizing God and submitting quietly to His will; in fact, it is flat rebellion against the Most High.

As we before remarked, all the persons whom we have just described, practically, if not advisedly, ignore the doctrine of God's continual working in the entire government of the world. Is it possible that thus either speaking or acting, they can really think in their hearts that the Lord God Omnipotent reigneth, and that He doeth all things well? At least there is room to doubt it. Should they deny the imputation, it rests with them under the circumstances either to prove that they do believe the doctrine of God's special providence, or to mend their ways. The latter course, we add in all charity, they will find the easier and the better.

We think that no one will deny, that the argument in support of God's special providence, derived from reason and experience, cannot be confuted. The voice of Revelation maintains it from first to last. It teaches that God takes a continual, active interest in the things of this world; that He is seen in history; that He rules in the affairs of men; and that all things work together eventually for good, in ultimate accordance with His will, and to the praise of His glory for whom all things were made. The Church, too, as she "affirms," as Dr. Hallam well remarks, "all truths and simply declares" what Scripture teaches, openly confesses this doctrine and avowedly lives by it. Her prayers are its complete exponent. Her ministers proclaim it to the people. It is therefore a necessary Christian doctrine—one that must be actually held.

Besides, the doctrine of God's special providence is a wholesome doctrine. It compels man to recognize the eternal omnipresence of God. It requires him to look up to God continually; to rely upon Him; to believe that His eye is over all His people; and that He will both reward and punish. It stimulates conscience. It brings into action and affords room for the development of man's best and highest powers. Finally, it energizes man to live the life he was designed to live—a life of faith, of prayer, of dependence upon his Heavenly Father; and it will induce him to "walk humbly with his God, and to run with patience the race that is set before him, looking unto Jesus." In the words of Bishop Taylor, "The *providence* of God is so great a *provider* for holy living and does so certainly minister to religion, that nature and chance, the order of the world, and the influences of heaven, are taught to serve the ends of the Spirit of God and the spirit of a man."

PRAYER.

As we write for those who profess to believe the truths of the Gospel, we deem it superfluous to adduce evidence either of the reasonableness or the Scripturalness of prayer to God. Indeed, the number of those who dispute the general proposition is too insignificant to claim our attention. We will, therefore, pursue our purpose, which is to set forth briefly the form, spirit, and matter of prayer.

Before entering upon these points we will elucidate one preliminary in regard to which some people find themselves singularly confused. It is this: To whom do we pray?—To which Person of the Godhead?—To all, or to God alone, in the abstract? We answer directly: There is but One God, and in the unity of God, there are Three Persons. Whoever prays to God, prays necessarily to each and all of the Three Persons: and whoever prays to each or all of the Three Persons, necessarily prays to the One God. No form can change the fact. Still it is necessary to pray understandingly. What the Church teaches on this subject may be gathered directly from the Litany. Observe the beginning where petitions are addressed to the Three Persons respectively in order, and then one to all combined. Mark, too, the threefold entreaty in the Minor Litany: "Lord have mercy upon us." "Christ have mercy upon us." "Lord have mercy upon us." Now this is not mere fervor or vehemence. It is in both cases a direct recognition of the Trinity—Three Persons and One God. This must not be forgotten. God the Father created us; God the Son redeemed us; God the Holy Ghost sanctifieth us. This is the economy of the Deity. Therefore we address the Three Persons individually; but we are not unmindful that there is only One God, and that we must all pray to Him, and do pray to Him only. "I will pray," says St. Paul, "with the spirit, and I will pray with the understanding also. Let all things be done to edifying."

Prayer is the generic term for communion with God. It is properly divided into two classes, viz., First, ORATIO, or extended prayer; second, PRECES, or short appeals. Each of these classes may be subdivided again. Each comprehends: 1. *Invocation*, or address to the Deity; 2. *Prayer*, or request for what we need or desire; 3. *Intercession*, or request for others; 4. *Deprecation*, or entreaty for special protection; 5. *Obsecration*, or earnest appeal on peculiar grounds; 6. *Supplication*, or beseeching for pardon. These subdivisions are more commonly found in the second class than in the first. Thus the Litany, which, except the Lord's Prayer, is composed of *Preces*, comprehends them all. Originally it was intended for a single and separate service, and was arranged to include everything that its nature would admit. For instance, the first four petitions contain the Invocation to the Triune God; the second six, the Deprecations; the third three, the Obsecrations; the residue, Intercessions and Supplications. Hence the minister, after reading the Litany, says, "Let us pray"—which is not a rubric as some suppose—and passes on from the *preces* to an *oratio*. At the close of the latter he returns to *preces*. These being finished, he again says "Let us pray," and concludes with the *orationes* prescribed.

Irrespective of mode or mere style, prayer involves four necessary and important premises. 1. Belief in God's special providence; 2. That it be made in the name of the Lord Jesus Christ; 3. Faith in Him; 4. That it be made in the right spirit. The first premise is indispensable; for, unless God answer prayer, it would be superfluous to pray; and it may be added that prayer is a concession of the point. The second premise should be self-evident to the Christian, and needs no apology. Once, however, we observed to a clergyman —not a churchman—that it seemed to us that the omission to ask in Christ's Name, noticeable sometimes in extempore prayers, rendered the whole prayer nugatory. "Oh," said he, "that is understood, of course."

In other words, in the opinion of persons making the omission, our blessed Lord can be "understood" like a word in grammar—taken for granted. It will be perceived that the argument against prayer is, on such ground, irrefragable. For if Christ may be "understood," the whole prayer may be so too. The conclusion is inevitable. But the Church has not so learned Christ. She requires that every prayer shall set forth distinctly that it is made in His Name, as He commanded. Only praying so is an answer promised, or can an answer be expected: and praying so an answer will be vouchsafed, for He has said, "Whatsoever ye shall ask in My Name, that will I do." The third premise—"Faith in Him"—rests on equally clear and stable grounds. Faith in Christ involves a full acceptance of Christ, and recognition of His Deity and humanity and what follows therefrom. Nothing in Christian life is possible without faith. Ask therefore "in faith, nothing wavering." In regard to the fourth and last premise—"The right spirit"—we answer that the right spirit will exhibit entire deference to the will of God,—"not my will but Thine be done,"—and contentment with the response, whatever that may be.

"He prayeth well who loveth well," says Coleridge. Faith is the active power, love the element of prayer. God is love. The highest love of which man is capable is love to God. Love to man is the reactive overflowing of God's love to man, for God is the fountain of love. He *is* love itself. Love, as Alford says, is "His essential being." Hence, "he that loveth not never knew God. He who is born of God, however, loves God, knows God, does God's will. God Himself, who first loved us, viz., in Christ His incarnate Son, begot in us that love which of moral necessity returns again to the Father, and of like necessity embraces our brethren also." Such is the perfect love which is the proper element of prayer. With such love faith will coëxist, for "faith worketh by love." Prayer so conditioned will be acceptable to God, and will receive its due reward.

> "Prayer ardent opens heaven, lets down a stream
> Of glory on the consecrated hour
> Of man in audience with the Deity."

If it be necessary to understand the true conditions of prayer, it is also important to know what to pray.* We do not refer now to public prayer or church worship. For that the Church has provided a liturgy which has come to be "accounted," as Alexander Knox prophesied, "the richest treasure, next to the canonical Scriptures, in the Christian Church." Except in peculiar exigencies, for which the bishops provide, there is

* Madame Guyon, in her work on Prayer, refers to the "*Prayer of Silence*—a prayer too deep for words. It is a state of the soul which does not speak, because it has nothing to ask. It has a consciousness of having God, and in the fulness and richness of its possession it rests; it is silent, it asks nothing more." This is sentiment. There is no such thing as silent prayer. All prayer is predicated upon man's need, and is made to obtain the supply of that need. Madame Guyon has mistaken the peace of God, a fruit of prayer, for prayer itself.

no occasion for going beyond the Prayer Book; and no one governed by sound judgment and good taste will exceed its limits. There is ample room in it for the loftiest intellect, the holiest and humblest spirit, to commune with God.

But aside from public worship, every one thinks that there should be some general rules for guidance in the consecrated moments of audience with Heaven. Beyond the Lord's Prayer, which should never be omitted, what we should pray may be divided into two parts, viz., 1. What we should pray against; 2. What we should pray for.

In reply to the first, or in explanation, we say, the Tempter. If the beginnings of sin should be eschewed, if the very "appearance of evil" should be avoided, with what just apprehension must not the Christian regard temptation? "Few persons," says a distinguished orator, "who have enjoyed the ordinary advantages of an education in this part of the world, few persons that have anything that can be called a virtuous home, are in great danger of being led astray by vice, when it stands before them in all its native deformity.

> It is a monster of such hideous mien,
> That to be hated needs but to be seen."

But who is safe from the Circean voice of Temptation? Temptation is not a hideous monster. It too often comes in a lovely form, clothed with grace and beauty, speaking with a silver voice, and calling to us when we are off our guard. That is what we first need to be protected from."

Temptation as surely precedes sin, as thought precedes action. It is like the pilot-fish of the shark. The importance which our Saviour attached to especial protection against this power, is brought out very clearly, by a collation of His three most important prayers. "Lead us not into temptation," is the most touching petition in the Lord's Prayer, the one which the hearts of all most quickly and tremblingly respond to. "I pray not that Thou shouldst take them out of the world, but that Thou shouldst keep them from the evil," is the prayer of our Saviour when interceding with the Father for His disciples. The first step in the Divine keeping is preservation from temptation. Again, our Lord when making supplication for Himself, says, "O My Father, if it be possible, let this cup pass from Me" —Spare Me this trial, this temptation. If Christ shrank, even apparently, from conflict with this monster, how much more must weak, sinful man recoil from the contest. Notwithstanding, we are assured that we will not be tempted beyond what we can bear. It requires, however, faith to receive this ; for, in many cases, temptation seems to be but the precursor of a fall. Man, we believe, would instinctively shrink from temptation, were it not ministered by the arch fiend himself, who knows just where and how, most efficiently to apply the lever for man's overthrow. His part is

"To work in close design by fraud or guile."

Man naturally dreads trial under all circumstances. It brings home to him his weakness. He sees the sad consequences which too often result from it, both to himself and to others. Well may he fear since Satan is the enemy. Faith is the only shield that can protect him; prayer the only weapon he should employ. With these the fiend can be successfully encountered. Meet the enemy then on the threshold and be strong, ever supplicating God "to strengthen such as do stand, and to comfort and help the weak-hearted, to raise up those who fall, and finally to beat down Satan under our feet." Thus triumphing with Christ over the first enemy, we will not have cause to fear the last.

What should we pray for? It is proper for us to make known all our honest wants to God, and to ask that they be supplied, if it be good for us. Not our will but His be done. He is the Judge. At the same time there is one Gift, precious above all the good gifts which God gives to man, that we should fervently pray for. It is God's Holy Spirit, whom God has promised to give to those who ask Him, believing. This gift comprehends all that we can desire, all that we can imagine, and more than we can deserve. Nothing can be added to the Holy Spirit. After redeeming us by Christ, in giving us His Holy Spirit God freely gives us all things. "O the depth of the riches of God!" Let us ever pray then for His Holy Spirit, and receive Him and cherish Him in our hearts. He is the Spirit of life.

Prayer is a correlative of repentance; not that repentance which is merely compunction for sin, but a fixed determination with God's help to struggle against sin. It must be remembered also that in Heaven's Chancery

> "There is no shuffling, there the action lies
> In his true nature; and we ourselves compelled,
> Even to the teeth and forehead of our faults,
> To give in evidence."

Hence when we pray we must truly confess and sincerely resolve to forsake our sins. Paley writes, "it hath been well said of prayer, that prayer will either make a man leave off sinning, or sin will make him leave off prayer." This is by no means the case. David's life, as exhibited in the Psalms as well as in the Book of Kings, was a course of sinning and repenting. Yet from beginning to end he continued to pray and thus triumphed at last. What was true of the Hebrew king is true of every fallen being who attempts to lead a Christian life. The argument is not in favor of sinning but of prayer. Happen what may, man should "pray always and not faint."

Prayer is the "coöperant of duty." We must work and pray. God will make allowance for our infirmities, but He will not accept an intentional half service. We are in covenant with Him; He will perform His part and He will require us to make good ours. Neither must we pray perfunctorily; but we must be "not slothful in the business, fervent in the spirit, serving the Lord. Our reward is with Him.

Among the benefits that ensue to the person who sincerely prays is the reactive influence produced by the act of devotion. Were the petitions offered rarely granted, this benefit, which always is conferred, would be of no small value. Many a troubled spirit, many a broken heart has received divine consolation from simple communion with God. Doubtless the holy calm thus attained is the best answer, perhaps the only answer, God can sometimes in wisdom make to supplications in distress. No one who has experienced the heavenly comfort will underrate the peace and joy which flow from the consecrated hour.

Christian life is at unity with itself; it is one. We refer not only to the ingrafted life of Christ, but to that life which is the exponent of the former. All our life then must be in union and attuned to harmony with Christ. Is it obvious that nothing which the Church prescribes for holy living, can be dispensed with, and too much importance cannot be attached to the apostolic injunction: *Be steadfast in prayer.* In the exquisite words of Montgomery:

> "Prayer is the Christian's vital breath,
> The Christian's native air;
> His watchword at the gates of death,
> He enters heaven by prayer."

DEATH.

THERE are words which seem calculated by their very tone to awaken peculiar emotions, to suggest special trains of thought. Perhaps this arises from the association of ideas, or from that accord between sound and sense which appertains in a more or less degree to the words of every language. Death is one of these words. Something like a chill creeps round the heart when the sound of it falls upon the ear. Instinctively man shudders at the thought of death.

> "Death is a fearful thing:
> —to die, and go we know not where;
> To lie in cold obstruction, and to rot;
> This sensible warm motion to become
> A kneaded clod; and the delighted spirit
> To bathe in fiery floods, or to reside
> In thrilling regions of thick-ribbèd ice:
> To be imprisoned in the viewless winds,
> And blown with restless violence about
> The pendent world; or to be worse than worst
> Of those, that lawless and uncertain thoughts
> Imagine howling!—'tis too horrible!"

It must be confessed this is a dark picture of the fate

which awaits all men. It is one to which an excited imagination gave birth in the mind of a weak man, apparently on the verge of the grave and horribly afraid to die. Nevertheless, though Claudio's delineation of the hereafter is hardly justifiable, death is almost universally conceded to be a "fearful thing." But is the alarm which it excites reasonable or well-founded? As death is the common lot, should there be an unwillingness to die?

The subject has two aspects—the one physical, the other moral. We will examine them in order.

The separation of the immortal part of man—the spirit—from the body of flesh is physical or ordinary death. The spirit departs to the place appointed for it to dwell in, until, upon the resurrection from the dead, it shall be called to inform a body which will be as enduring as itself; the body composed of various elements maintained in high forms of chemical combination dissolves away. Corruption is merely a reduction of the elements from the highest to the lowest forms of combination. The inexplicable force, life, compels the one; death naturally ensures the other. It is the same throughout all creation wherein is life, whether sentient or non-sentient. Man can make an excellent copy of an animal or a plant; but he cannot endow it with life. The chemists can compose blood or sap which will be very fair counterfeit-presentments; but he cannot make them circulate. Life only can do that. Life only can bring a function into action or preserve it in activity.

It is a power which comes from God. It is a force which he gives. He gives it only for a season. When the unseen power is withdrawn, both animal and plant must corrode. There is a limit fixed for the duration of everything wherein is life. All that lives must die.

As life is of the highest importance in the physical economy of God, both plant and animal have been so fitted that each seeks its own preservation. The plant elevates its stem and expands its leaves to breathe the air and receive the light, and sends down its roots in pursuit of the sustenance which it craves. So persistent is it in its endeavors to effect its purposes that it assumes divers shapes and triumphs over singular obstacles. So pertinacious is it in its efforts to live, that, as far as in it lies, it refuses to die. The animal, too, is gifted from above with an especial instinct of self-preservation, and avoids death as his most terrible enemy. Surmounting dangers, sustaining injuries, surviving disease, he lives out his allotted days. Man, the head of the animal creation, though his instincts are much inferior to those of subordinate creatures, has the instinct of self-preservation well developed. Perhaps it is even increased by the influence of his higher nature. Man, therefore, naturally shuns death. It is only when supported by decided courage and fortitude, or nerved by some inspiring principle, that he evinces a disregard of death, an indifference to life. We refer, of course, to those who possess the *mens sana in corpore sano.*

Physical death—we refer to it in connection with man—may proceed either from the exhaustion of the living power consequent upon old age—which is infrequent; or it may result from violence or disease. It may exhibit itself first in any part of the body and progress by inches; but it is perfected in the brain. That organ being the centre and source of vital force, unless through its nervous system it excite the heart into motion, there can be no circulation of the blood, no action of the lungs to aërate the life-bearing stream. As long, too, as the brain does exert an adequate force, the heart and lungs, if uninjured, must perform their joint functions. If they cease their action, the arterialization ceases, and the brain, deprived of blood, must perish from atrophy. Thus the natural as well as the complex body (the Church) "fitly joined together and compacted by that which every joint supplieth, according to the effectual working in the measure of every part, maketh increase of the body." Life apparently terminates when the chest ceases to act. This cessation, however, may be only temporary, as in cases of *syncope* or *asphyxia*, or it may be simulated. Inaction of the chest, therefore, is not certain, though it generally is very good evidence of death. The latter cannot be absolutely predicated to have ensued until vitality has departed from the brain. Then and not until then does the spirit—the *hospes comesque corporis*—leave the house of flesh to soar away.

"Animula vagula blandula,
Hospes comesque corporis;
Quæ nunc abibis in loca,
Pallidula rigida nidula
Nec ut soles dabis jocos?"

Much has been written on the question of misapprehension in regard to death and premature interment. There is no difficulty about the matter. When certain spots appear upon the abdomen every doubt is removed; death has done its work. Generally, however, there are signs familiar to all medical men, which are unmistakable and which precede the inevitable sign and undoubted proof we have mentioned.

The act of dying is not attended with pain. Even when consciousness is maintained, as is often the case, to the moment of dissolution, pain is not experienced. That is incident, in a greater or less degree, to the evils of the flesh. In consequence of injuries or disease some persons die agonizing deaths. No such suffering must be confounded with what is termed the "agony," or imaginary violent rending in twain of the spirit and the flesh. Fear of the article of death—physical death purely—can arise only from ignorance or undue timidity. There is no pain in it as such. Indeed, very often the approach of death, where great suffering has been experienced from the nature of the disease, is signalized by a release from all pain so completely that the sign of death is mistaken for a sign of recovery, and the patient, amid the delusive hopes that have been awakened in the breasts of friends, passes away like a "chris-tom child." The parting of the spirit is as quiet and noiseless as was its coming. St. Paul well describes it when he says of David that "he fell on sleep."

The ancient Hebrews had a tradition that an angel called Samael was the prince of death, and that he came and bore away the spirits of the dying to their new abode. The Mussulmans, who doubtless borrowed the idea from the Hebrews, attribute the same part to Azrael. The idea is not less fanciful than that of the Greek poets, who make, in their mythology, Death and Sleep twin sisters, and the daughters of Night. The association is natural, and conceived in the spirit of poetry. Krummacher has elaborated the idea in a parable which is so beautiful that we venture to translate it, though it must lose some of its charm in the rendering. It is as follows:

"The Angels of Sleep and Death in brotherly companionship were wandering over the earth. It was evening. They threw themselves down to rest upon a hill not far from the habitations of men. A melancholy silence reigned around, broken only by the sound of the vesper-bell in the distant village. Mute and quiet, as is their custom, the two beneficent guardian-angels of mankind sat in affectionate embrace. Night drew on. Suddenly the Angel of Sleep arose from his mossy couch, and with a light hand scattered the invisible seeds of slumber. The evening wind bore them to the quiet abode of the weary husbandmen. Sweet sleep began now to embrace the inhabitants of the several cottages, from the gray-headed old man who leaned upon his staff to the infant in the cradle. The sick forgot their pains, the mourners their grief, the poor their cares. Every eye slept. Soon, after his task was finished, the benevolent Angel laid himself down again alongside of his stern brother.—'When the morning dawns,' exclaimed he, with cheerful innocence, 'the world will praise me as its friend and benefactor! O what joy to do good in secret! How happy are we invisible messengers of good spirits! How beautiful is our silent calling!'—Thus spake the friendly Angel of Sleep. The Angel of Death looked at him with quiet sadness, and a tear, such as immortals shed, stood in his large dark eye. 'Alas,' said he, 'I cannot, as you, enjoy the thanks of the grateful; the world calls me its enemy and the destroyer of its peace!'—'O my Brother,' responded the Angel of Sleep, 'will not the good at their awakening recognize and bless thee as their friend? Are we not Brothers and Messengers of the same Father?'—As he thus spake the eye of the Angel of Death glistened, and the two brother-spirits tenderly embraced each other!"

The moral aspect of death awakens other considerations. Conscious of immortality, aware of sin, advertised of a judgment to come, man shrinks from the ordeal he is doomed to undergo. He clings to the life he knows, be it what it may; he would not die; Death is to him the king of terrors. The mass of men, we apprehend, do not dread death as the *end* of life. There is no "inward horror of falling into naught"; the "soul startles at destruction" only in the imagination of the poet. On the contrary, we believe that if annihilation were the sanction of law, the reward of sin, periodical deluges would be necessary to purify the earth and stay God's repentance for having made man. No, it is not the "longing after immortality" which causes sinful man to wish to live, live on, to never die; it is the thought of the hereafter.

> "To die;—to sleep;—
> To sleep! perchance to dream; aye, there's the rub;
> For in that sleep of death what dreams may come,
> When we have shuffled off this mortal coil,
> Must give us pause."

The same pen which traced Claudio's fear of death here explains the cause of all such alarm. It is the dread of the hereafter. But faith, reflection, courage, serve to modify, if they do not altogether remove this natural apprehension. Thus there are some who, though touched by a solemn awe, do not fear to die.

From the New Testament we learn that there are two deaths—the first and the second death. The one refers to death in the ordinary acceptation of the word, the other to the punishment reserved for the impenitent. "Physical death" says Alford, "is so subordinate to spiritual death that it often hardly comes into account with the writers of the New Testament; it is overlooked and disregarded in comparison with that which is really death." (Cf. John xi. 25–6, with Eph. ii. 2.)

A proper consideration of our subject leads to the inquiry: What do we know of the world to come?—We only know what has been explicitly revealed and what follows logically therefrom. For example, we know that at the appointed time the spirit sloughs off its fleshly integument, and in its unclothed state goes to the place of departed spirits, there to remain until the resurrection, when it will be united to the spiritual body and the entire organization perfected. Man will then be a full man, possessing body, soul and spirit, all equally immortal. The nature of the body with which the spirit is to be clothed on the resurrection-day we are utterly unable to explain. St. Paul says there is a spiritual body—*pneumatikos*, controlled by the spirit, not *psuchikos*, controlled by the animal soul; but the specific character of that body has not been revealed. We may assume safely, however, that it will be such that the identity of each individual will be completely and consciously preserved. We know farther that there will be two resurrections. "Blessed are they who have part in the first resurrection." They are the "dead in Christ" whom the Lord will bring with Him to meet the saints on earth who shall be "changed," when He comes to reign a thousand years. A certain space after the millennium the second resurrection will take place and will comprehend all who had no part in the first. Then will come the judgment. They who shall be found to possess faith in Jesus Christ—among such of course will be they who had part in the first resurrection—will be pardoned and rewarded according to their works. The measure of the latter is concealed. Doubtless, age, capacity, circumstance, grace, will be taken into account. God is just. They who shall not be found on the great day shielded by faith in Jesus Christ will be consigned to the second death. Of the form, mode, character of the life hereafter we know as little as of the body which is to take part in it, whether that life shall be to live with Christ or to die with Satan. All we can say is, that the former will receive "those things which God has prepared for them that love Him, which pass man's comprehension, and exceed all he can either desire or deserve;" the latter will depart into "everlasting darkness." How vast the reward! How fearful the punishment! Light and life on the one hand, death and darkness on the other. How great the contrast! But, "shall not the Judge of all the earth do right?" That Judge will be the God-Man Jesus Christ our Lord.

National character is often illustrated by the characteristic expressions in use on the subject of death. Thus, says De Vere, "the poetical Greek called his burying place, such as it was, a *koimeterion*, or 'sleeping place;' the faith of the Hebrew spoke in his *beth-haim*, or 'house of the living!' The proud Roman avoided the very name of what was to him, but too often, mere annihilation; he did not like to die, but called it *vitam suam mutare*, 'to change his life,' *transire a seculo*, 'to pass from the age,' or *si quid de eo humanitus contigerit*, 'if anything human hath happened to him.'" The Romans, too, frequently used the expression *abiit ad plures*, he "has joined the majority." It was a fashionable phrase rife among the wits, probably, at the baths. "The French of our day," continues De Vere, "shows, with regard to death, that peculiar feature in the national character which dislikes being disturbed by unpleasant impressions in the enjoyment of life, and most admires ingenious delicacy in avoiding all directness by euphemistic terms. The word *mort*, 'dead,' is but rarely heard in France; it has an icy breath about it, which the Frenchman avoids as a bad omen, like the Roman of old; the odor of death he changes into an *odeur du sapin*, 'scent of the fir;' he prefers the *char funèbre*, 'funeral car,' to the *corbillard*, 'hearse,' *trépas* and *décès*, 'demise' and 'decease,' to straight-forward terms, and the English 'corpse' is to him a simple *corps*. The genius of the language bends to his whims and fancies so far as to allow him to speak of *mourir tout en vie*, and even to say *se mourir* (the two latter phrases cannot be rendered into equivalent English), as if death was nothing but a voluntary act chosen at will. Highly poetical and slightly transcendental appear, on the other hand, the German *Friedhof*, 'peace-yard,' and *Gottesacker*, 'God's field,' which gradually find their way into other idioms also." Americans are not without their specialities in these matters. "Corpse" and "body" are almost superseded by "remains;" "dead" is left to the Bible and liturgy; and in imitation of Paris and the Père la Chaise, the Saxon "grave-yard" and "church-yard" are rapidly disappearing in the more elegant "rural cemetery" or the peculiar appellation of each "necropolis," or beautiful abode of departed friends, where, amid lovely situations, charming prospects, and fashionable avenues, we are tempted to reverse the words of the minister and exclaim, "In the midst of death we are in life."

Death often elucidates individual characteristics. Proximity to it frequently unfolds the man. What is singular, there is sometimes either a presentiment or an absolute conviction that death is near at hand, which nothing can dispel or shake, and which in many cases proves correct. Nelson is said to have experienced the former, and the latter is familiar to physicians generally. What increases a natural awe on the subject of death is that it is a solitary act. It is a way which must be travelled alone. Nor does it in any way alter the fact, that one may apparently depart with a large company to join the ever-increasing "majority." The Roman sentinel who perished at his post when Vesuvius overwhelmed Pompeii; the soldier who fell among thousands on the field of Austerlitz; the seaman who was engulfed with the ill-fated President; the man who breathes his last in the arms of friends, the recipient of every attention, the object of solicitude and affection—

each one goes on his way alone. "Thy rod and Thy staff" are the only stays granted to man, from the peasant to the statesman, when he "walks through the valley of the shadow of death."

Cæsar says:

> "Cowards die many times before their deaths;
> The valiant never taste of death but once.
> Of all the wonders that I yet have heard,
> It seems to me most strange that men should fear;
> Seeing that death, a necessary end,
> Will come, when it will come."

But, whatever may have been the fear of death manifested through life, as a rule, it is greatly modified or disappears when the inevitable call comes. Doctor Johnson is a striking example of this. Possessing unquestionable courage, both moral and physical, endowed with great intellectual powers, thoroughly informed upon the subject of religion, deeply convinced of the truth of Christianity, and through the Church availing himself of all the means appointed for the attainment of salvation, he nevertheless exhibited from youth to old age an awful horror of death. He took no pains to conceal it. Yet, says his biographer, "when he approached to his awful change, his mind became tranquil, and he exibited as much fortitude as becomes a thinking man in that situation." He died with entire composure and resignation.

Some writers regard the composure generally exhibited by the dying, as merely an index of the controlling power of vanity. They say, man will play his last part well whenever he has spectators; we know not how he would die alone, without a reporter. We admit that vanity is a powerful element in human character, and that many acts both good and bad are inspired by this feeling. But we believe, also, that there are other reasons which explain the phenomenon of man's ordinarily making a quiet end. 1. Physical debility, with which the mind sympathizes; when dying becomes like falling asleep through exhaustion. 2. Courage, which apparently nothing can pale, which not only rises itself, but prompts man to concentrate all his powers to meet the emergency. 3. Divine aid; in other words, God, knowing the weakness of man, enables him to die, as He has enabled him to live. 4. Faith in Christ, which is both sword and shield, an unfailing weapon and a sure defence. Perhaps other reasons might be adduced, such as faith in human nature, insensibility, ignorance; but they are of little importance, and need not delay us.

Numerous are the deathbed scenes which have been recounted for the warning, amusement, and edification of the living—some of them deplorable, like those of Buckingham, Savage, and Sheridan: some of them partially manufactured, as that of Addison: some of them curious and characteristic, as that of Playfair, who asked that the "Principia" might be read to him to soothe his pain; or as that of Dr. Adam, who dismissed the class, to die; or as that of Charles II, who apologized for keeping the company waiting: some of them solemn and affecting; such as many have witnessed: and some wellnigh sublime. We might fill pages in endeavoring to relate them. Woolsey cried, "If I had served my God as I have my king, He would not have abandoned me." Philip II exclaimed, "Oh that I had never reigned!" Randolph screamed, "Remorse—write in on a card, let me *see* it." Whitefield died "silent," having said previously that he should do so, "as he had witnessed for God during his life." Washington's death was extraordinary. Constitutionally brave, after a life of duty, "having the testimony of a good conscience, in the communion of the Catholic Church, in the confidence of a certain faith, in the comfort of a reasonable, religious, and holy hope," and, we doubt not, "in favor with God and in perfect charity with the world, he was gathered unto his fathers." Feeling that he was about to depart, he placed his finger upon the left pulse, and quietly and calmly numbered the time of the ebbing current, until at the last beat the massive hands fell lifeless apart. It is said that no one ever knew the exact moment he fell asleep, or the precise second his spirit took wing. If any man ever did realize it, that man was Washington.

We return to the question—Is a fear of death just and well founded? The "sense" of physical death, as we have intimated, is all "in apprehension." Not so is the case with death in a moral point of view. They who are out of Christ—through whom only can they be in covenant with God—and therefore utterly unprepared to die, in view of the dark future that impends, may well say in the words of Claudio:

> "The weariest and most loathed worldly life,
> That age, ache, penury, and imprisonment
> Can lay on nature, is paradise
> To what we fear of death."

This is the effect of sin; this is the dread of the second death. "The death of Christ," however, as Alford remarks, "having brought to nought the agency of the devil in death, because that death of His, being not the penalty of His own sin, but the atoning sacrifice for the sin of the world, all those who by faith are united to Him can now look on death no longer as the penalty of sin, but only as the passage for them, as it was for Him, to a new and glorious life of triumph and blessedness." Hence it follows, that while to the unprepared death must be a fearful thing, to the prepared it may be considered as a good. Man need not fear to die.

It is evident, however, that a preparation for death is necessary, lest it prove an evil and not a good. It remains then to inquire what is the most fitting preparation for the inevitable journey which all must take. Undoubtedly the best preparation for death is a right life. When Socrates was pressed by his friend Hermogenes to make ready for his defence, "What!" said he, "my Hermogenes, suppose you that I have not spent all my life in preparing for this very thing?" Hermogenes desiring that he would explain himself:

"I have," continued he, "steadily persisted, throughout life, in a diligent endeavor to do nothing which is unjust; and this I take to be the best and most honorable preparation." Montaigne writes: "He who would teach men to die, would teach them to live." The question of dying clearly returns to one of living. Such being the case, it is apparent that man should so live that he will have no more to apprehend from death than what properly accords with a just fear of the Lord. For as God has instituted love as a power to incline the heart to good, so He has prescribed fear as a force to deter from sin. Both work together to the benefit of man and praise of God.

But what rules for living rightly can be laid down? Simply these: Believe in the Lord Jesus Christ and keep His commandments. The latter are chiefly two. The first exacts love to God; the second, love to man's fellow man. The one involves the honoring of God in all the requirements of His holy Church; the other—a consequence of the first, and lifeless without it—demands that man be warm-hearted and true-hearted. These are, it is true, great general principles; but from them, rules of action to meet every phase of life may be deduced. No one need err therein. The only commentary necessary is the Golden Rule. This will settle every question of construction that can arise.

Jeremy Taylor, who has written so admirably on "Holy Living" as the proper precursor to "Holy Dying," says: "In the morning, when you awake, accustom yourself to think first upon God, or something in order to His service; and at night also let Him close thine eyes, and let your sleep be necessary and healthful, not idle and expensive of time, beyond the needs and conveniences of nature; and sometimes be curious to see the preparation which the sun makes, when he is coming forth from his chambers of the east." Sir Matthew Hale, the able lawyer and upright judge, whom Washington took for a model, and whose letters he so much admired, "divided himself," says Burnet, "between the duties of religion and the studies of his profession; in the former he was so regular, that for six and thirty years' time, he never once failed going to church on the Lord's day; he took a strict account of his time, of which the reader will best judge by the scheme he drew for a diary. It is set down in the same simplicity in which he writ it for his own private use.

"MORNING.—To lift up my heart to God in thankfulness for renewing my life.

"EVENING.—Cast up the accounts of the day. If aught amiss, beg pardon. Gather resolution of more vigilance. If well, bless the mercy and grace of God that hath supported thee."

But the variety that exists in age, character, calling, capacity, means, renders it impossible to prescribe formulas adapted to all men. General principles and the self-evident rules that flow from them are all that can be set down on paper. As regards the rest, each man must see to it for himself. The Church, with the Bible and Prayer Book, certainly offers all the instruction that can possibly be necessary.

In regard to the practice of life in this world, an error is prevalent, which is productive of evil and needs correction. It is the confounding the service with the worship of God. The former properly comprehends all man's life; the latter, only communion with God. For instance: man serves God in every part of his life, when he is honestly performing his duty in that station of life in which it has pleased God to call him. The better, the more efficiently he executes his calling, the better he serves God. It is idle to suppose that God placed man in this world to eat his bread in the sweat of his brow, and endowed him with genius, talents, and industry to illustrate and adorn the world he inhabits, and then counts it sin in him to use his heaven-born faculties, to develop his mind and body, to unfold and exemplify nature and art in all their variety, beauty, and perfection, if he do not cast contempt upon all the things of this world and devote all his thoughts and time to doing that which it is revealed is the occupation of the saints in heaven. "We have not so learned Christ." God has given all that he has given to be used; but not to be abused. There is no position, no wealth, no honor, which the world offers, that man may not strive for, nay, should not strive for, and, if successful, enjoy, provided he does all in subordination to the love and fear of God. What would man be, what would this earth be, were it not so? The one an animal, the other a desert. God wills that man should employ all his faculties and opportunities directly for his own benefit and that of his fellow man, and thus to His glory. To energize him, He has tied honors, rewards, blessings to the path of this life; and He has also strewn some thorns in the way, that man may not think only of this life and lose sight of the next and of Him. God is not God of the dead either in body, soul, or spirit, but of the living, whom He will have to live neither abjectly nor in slavish fear of their Creator, but earnestly, with high purpose and generous confidence. Thus He will get himself honor upon the work of His hands. Every man should serve God with the best that he hath, not only generally, but particularly, as the case may require, asking and hoping for blessing here and salvation hereafter. A depreciation of man derogates from God; but the elevation of man under God redounds to the glory of Christ.

But the worship of God must not be neglected. A specific portion of man's time is due to this observance. The Church is the public medium for it. She has appointed the Lord's Day in honor of her Head, to be kept, analogously to the Hebrew Sabbath, as a day of rest, wherein man may repose from ordinary avocations and specially and publicly worship God. She has also appointed other times and seasons for the same purpose; and she further strictly enjoins that every one should constantly and habitually worship God in private, not only in connection with the family where that is possible, but separately and secretly. There is no exception. No excuse can be offered for a neglect of either public or private devotion. If any one aver that his necessary avocations deprive him of time and opportunity, let him consider the examples of Sir Matthew Hale and of Washington. The first was engrossed in the labors of an arduous profession; the second wellnigh overwhelmed with the duties incident to his exalted position; yet both were churchmen, both found time to remember God in public and in private. It is a question of inclination. Where that exists, the duty will be performed. Be it remembered, too, that work is not worship, as the enemies of Christ assume. Worship is specific communion with God through Christ, and involves the devotion of particular times and seasons to that service. Should a man so involve himself in the affairs which appertain exclusively to this life that he can spare no time to commune with God, he will yet have to find time to die. When that event shall arrive, he will, perhaps unavailingly, regret that he has robbed God of the few hours which He asked of him while here; that he had not taken time to live as one who must die.

Let no one fondly imagine that after a life passed in forgetfulness of death and of God, he will be able at the last moment to turn and repent. Deathbed repentance is possible, but it is very improbable. God alone can tell whether it is sincere or the mere result of physical depression or of nervous trepidation.

Commentators say that Holy Scripture affords but one instance (the penitent thief), that none might "despair," and only one, that none might "presume."

The sum of the matter is, the only reliable preparation for death is a life of faith in Christ, confirmed by a performance of duty to God and man—a life passed in the service and worship of God. The man who thus passes through life, "building himself up in his most holy faith," and, in all his service and worship of mind and body, ever "looking unto Jesus as the Leader and Perfecter of his faith," when the summons, which comes to cottage and to castle, comes to call him away, he will not dread the sound, he will not fear to die. Death will be to him merely the door by which he shall enter into the rest which the Saviour has prepared by His mighty work for those that love Him and keep His commandments.

> "So live that when the summons comes to join
> The innumerable caravan, which moves
> To that mysterious realm, where each shall take
> His chamber in the silent halls of death,
> Thou go not, like the quarry slave at night,
> Scourged to his dungeon, but, sustained and soothed
> By an unfaltering trust, approach thy grave
> Like one who wraps the drapery of his couch
> About him, and lies down to pleasant dreams."

O Lord, from whom all good things do come; grant to us, thy humble servants, that by thy holy inspiration we may think those things that are good, and by thy merciful guiding may perform the same, through our Lord Jesus Christ. *Amen.*

www.ingramcontent.com/pod-product-compliance
Lightning Source LLC
LaVergne TN
LVHW011237110826
845150LV00006B/1663

* 9 7 8 1 4 2 5 5 1 4 8 5 3 *